THE COMPLETE GUIDE TO THE SHIBA INU

Vanessa Richie

LP Media Inc. Publishing

www.lpmedia.org

Publication Data

Vanessa Richie

The Complete Guide to the Shiba Inu---- First edition.

Summary: "Successfully raising a Shiba Inu dog from puppy to old age" --- Provided by publisher.

ISBN: 978-1-952069-06-2

[1. Shiba Inu --- Non-Fiction] I. Title.

This book has been written with the published intent to provide accurate and authoritative information in regard to the subject matter included. While every reasonable precaution has been taken in preparation of this book the author and publisher expressly disclaim responsibility for any errors, omissions, or adverse effects arising from the use or application of the information contained inside. The techniques and suggestions are to be used at the reader's discretion and are not to be considered a substitute for professional veterinary care. If you suspect a medical problem with your dog, consult your veterinarian.

Design by Sorin Rădulescu

First paperback edition, 2019

Cover Photo Courtesy of Inger Lise Fløtten

TABLE OF CONTENTS

INTRODUCTION

CHAPTER 1

CHAPTER 2

CHAPTER 3

CHAPTER 15

CHAPTER 16

CHAPTER 17

CHAPTER 18

INTRODUCTION

Shiba Inu are one of the most easily recognized dog breeds in the world, though you would be forgiven for mistaking them for domesticated foxes. One of the six dog breeds indigenous to Japan, they became popular following the end of World War II when the breed nearly became extinct. Today, they are on nearly every continent on Earth. While Shiba Inu have always remained a popular breed in Japan, much of the rest of the world has since learned to love this adorable, very strong-willed breed.

They are considered medium sized, but they are definitely on the smaller side of that scale. This makes them fantastic dogs for any environment. Their double layered coat means that they prefer somewhat colder climates, and they shed a considerable amount during the warmer months. This is a breed that is fairly easy to groom, with more brushing needed during the warm months. You won't need to bathe your Shiba often as their coats are resistant to dirt.

Shiba Inu are incredibly intelligent, a reflection of thousands of years working with humans. Their propensity for escaping means that you can't leave this dog outside alone for any amount of time. Furthermore, if you don't properly train them, they will get bored. This typically manifests itself in destructive behavior. That said, Shiba Inu are not an easy breed to train, making them a poor choice for first time dog owners. Despite their strong-willed nature though, the Shiba Inu can be an incredibly loving and loyal companion for families who know how to handle intelligent breeds.

The dogs are incredibly fast and are great participants in agility competitions. They are equally happy to explore new areas with you, making them great travel companions. While they aren't known for their fondness for strangers, the dogs don't tend to be aggressive. Shiba Inu have a long history of chasing prey. This is why they are so agile today, and it also means you have to be a bit more cautious when you go outside.

Given their very long history, the Shiba Inu are surprisingly healthy. They are not prone to many genetic ailments, though dysplasia and eye problems are common in the breed. Their life span is between 12 and 16 years, meaning if you take good care of your Shiba Inu, you will probably have more than a decade of companionship together.

Photo Courtesy of
Rachel Deihl

CHAPTER 1
One Of The Best Recognized Asian Breeds

Japan gave rise to one of the most easily recognizable dogs in the world – the Shiba Inu. At a glance, you could easily mistake one of these dogs for a fox as they have the same coloring and are roughly the same size. They are also incredibly intelligent and won't listen to someone who has not gained their respect. These dogs have been a part of human civilizations since the Jomon Period.

*Photo Courtesy of
Joseph Hsu
Instagram @joeshoe*

From The Jomon – Six Famous Japanese Breeds

Despite being small, Japan is the origin of six notable dog breeds:

- Shiba Inu (the smallest of the six)
- Shikoku
- Kishu
- Kai
- Hokkaido
- Akita (the largest of the six)

If you do a quick search on each of these dog breeds, what you will probably notice right off the bat is that they all have a similar appearance. The one that looks the most unique is the Kai, largely because of its brindle coat and tail. Despite these differences, you can tell that the six breeds came from a small genetic pool. The primary difference is their size, indicating the work they did over the centuries. For example, the large and well known Akita was once used to help hunt larger game. The Hokkaido is thought to be one of the oldest dog breeds in the world (and certainly in Japan). The Shiba Inu was bred to hunt smaller animals.

Behind The Name

FUN FACT
National Shiba Club
of America (NSCA)

The National Shiba Club of America (NSCA), established in 1992, is the national organization for promoting the best interests of the Shiba Inu breed in America. Members of the NSCA agree to abide by a code of ethics and must be in good standing with the American Kennel Club. The NSCA has member clubs across the nation and maintains a breeder directory at its website, www.shibas.org.

Unlike some of the other Japanese breeds, the meaning of the Shiba Inu's name is less clear. The second half, Inu, is easy enough – it's the Japanese word for dog. The term Shiba, though, could refer to one of at least two different aspects of the dog's history. The first explanation is fairly straightforward; shiba means "brushwood" in Japanese. This could describe the color of the dog's coat (brushwood is a similar reddish color in the fall) or be an indication of the breed's occupation. Because of their size, Shiba Inu hunted smaller animals in the shrubs. The second possible origin of the word shiba comes from Japan's Nagano prefecture, where the term simply means "little."

Regardless of what the name's true origin might be, both are accurate ways of describing this adorable little pup.

*Photo Courtesy of
Whitney Kono*

Photo Courtesy of
Inger Lise Fløtten

A Diligent Partner In The Hunt

The presence of dogs in Japan goes all the way back to 7,000 BC, known as the Jomon Period. In the Chronicles of Japan, dogs are noted as being instrumental in helping people survive on the island. It is thought that the Shiba Inu was established by 300 BC, helping people living in and around the mountains of the island.

Between 1603 and 1867 CE, Japan began to import dogs from all around the world, which helped to change the appearance and temperament of some of the breeds. For the next 50 years, breeding with other dogs and the popularity of these new breeds began to push out the traditional Japanese dogs. The Japanese breeds that had once been essential to the island suffered a steep decline in numbers. As a result, some Japanese people began to fear that the native Japanese dogs would become extinct, and a movement to protect the six breeds began to form during the early part of the 20th century. The Japanese Education Ministry designated the different breeds as national treasures. Despite this effort, the reduced number of dogs saw nearly all of them become extinct after World War II.

The Toll Of World War Ii And Saving Shiba Inu From Extinction

The timing of the effort to save the Shiba Inu is perhaps what ultimately helped to save them.

Photo Courtesy of
Caitlin Rubinstein

Prior to World War II, there were three types of Shiba Inu, named after their specific geographical region:

- Mino
- Sanin
- Shinshu

During the war, many dogs were killed during bombing raids. Many of those that survived the bombings died because of the virus distemper, which is highly contagious in canines. Thanks to some breeding programs that were in place prior to the war, the Japanese were able to save this adorable little dog from entirely disappearing. Breeders scoured the most remote parts of the country to find some of the last remaining Mino and Sanin. With too few left to breed, it was best to mix the three variants together to ensure there were minimal genetic issues. Today's Shiba is a result of those breeding efforts between the various original Shiba Inu types.

With many American servicemen stationed in Japan, an interest in the Shiba Inu began to grow. When a serviceman took a Shiba Inu home with him in 1954, the breed started to gain a lot of attention. It was recognized by the American Kennel Club in 1992. Today, Shiba are the most popular dog in Japan, and were named the 50th most popular breed in the US in 2012.

The Loyalty Of The Shiba Inu

One of the reasons that people are willing to put up with an intelligent dog that has a fierce independent streak is that they are an incredibly loyal dog. They are able to help solve problems and will stick with you when you need them most.

Most people have heard the story of the Akita who waited for his human every day at the train station years after his person died. The Shiba Inu have been in a more recent true story that proves that they are incredibly loyal and loving of their family. Following the Yamakoshi earthquake in Japan in 2004, one Shiba Inu was able to get out of the rubble. She got her puppies out of the dangerous structure, ensuring that they were fine. Next, she went in to find her person, an elderly man trapped under the rubble. She woke him up and drew attention to his location as the man worked to get out from the rubble. He was then airlifted from the region. When he was finally able to return a couple of weeks later, the Shiba Inu and her puppies had managed to survive and remained healthy under the less than ideal circumstances.

CHAPTER 2
Looks Like A Fox, Acts Like A Cat, Loves Like A Dog

Between appearance, temperament, and personality, the Shiba Inu is a unique combination of several animals. The physical appearance makes you think of a fox. The way a Shiba Inu will look disinterestedly at you during training will definitely remind you of a cat. And when it comes to family, a Shiba will love you just as much as any dog. While they are certainly small, they have a big dog personality.

The Defining Physical Characteristics Of The Shiba Inu

FUN FACT
Insta-Shiba Inu

Maru Taro is perhaps the internet's most famous Shiba Inu. With over two million followers on Instagram, this adorable Shiba Inu lives in Japan with his owner, Shinjiro Ono. You can follow the adventures of this fluffy, loveable dog on Instagram @marutaro, where he has a verified account.

The Shiba Inu is a compact, well-built little dog, weighing 20 lbs. on average, with males averaging around 22 lbs. and females weighing around 18 lbs. They stand about a foot tall at their shoulders, so they are about knee height on most adults.

Most of them are a reddish color, though there are variations, with some dogs being black and tan instead of red or red sesame. This is a result of the interbreeding of the three Shiba Inu variations. The dogs have two coats, which gives them a lush, fluffy look, rather like a stuffed animal.

A Shiba's face is small and round, with intelligent eyes and triangular ears. When they aren't assessing the world around them, the dogs tend to have a little smile on their face, which often turns into a look of happiness as they are interacting with their family and having fun.

Health Problems Common To Shiba Inu

Despite their long history, the Shiba Inu are an incredibly healthy breed. The biggest health concerns aren't life threatening, and are covered in more detail in Chapter 17.

What you will need to watch for are signs of hip dysplasia, patellar luxation, and a range of eye issues. This is also a breed that tends to have environmental allergies, scratching and biting at their bodies. Check out Chapters 6 and 16 for details on inhalant allergies.

Some Shiba Inu have dental problems, but you can avoid many of these by being proactive with dental care (Chapter 15).

Photo Courtesy of Brooke Steinbach

Independence Disclaimer – They Are Intelligent And Confident

"Shibas are independent and intelligent, stubborn, tough, active (with lots of energy), escape artists, and drama queens (both male and female)."

Susan Norris-Jones
SunJo Shiba Inu & Japanese Chin

One of the biggest problems that Shiba Inu parents face is having an intelligent dog that simply does not want to listen. There is a good reason why the Shiba Inu are often compared to cats – they have a similar independent streak and aren't clingy or interested in being the center of attention all of the time. When they want attention, they will seek it out, but, otherwise, they may not be in the mood to play with you when you feel like it.

They have unlimited confidence, and for good reason. With their quick intellect, they can usually assess a situation and figure out how best to use what is at hand to accomplish a goal.

This is a breed that will spend a considerable amount of time self-cleaning, which is nice for you, and is another way that the dogs are like cats. They want their bodies and homes clean, which is why they are so easy to housetrain (and why they can give you a false sense of how easy they are to train).

Photo Courtesy of Alayne Levine

A Loving And Alert Family Dog

"The Shiba Inu has come a long way from having a reputation of being aggressive and not good around children, to now being known as a very playful and loving companion."

Jan Hill
Dark Knight Shibas

In spite of their size, Shiba can be great watch dogs. All you have to do is a quick video search to see that this is not a quiet breed. They have many different noises and sounds that they use to let you know how they are feeling.

What makes them great apartment dogs and good watch dogs is that they don't tend to bark at every noise. They are alert and attentive, so if there is a noise that causes concern, they will let you know. They may also make noise, including barking, when they are playing or angry. Just like you tend to get louder when you are feeling either really excited or angry, the Shiba Inu can be very expressive and vocal when they feel extreme emotions.

Some Shiba sound like they are yodeling or talking back, which can be incredibly entertaining. Perhaps one of the most alarming sounds they make is their scream, usually when they're attempting to get your attention to play.

May Be Too Much Dog For Novice Dog Owners

"The Shiba Inu is not for the inexperienced dog owner. Looks are very deceiving!"

CJ Strehle
JADE Shiba Inu

Photo Courtesy of Karolina Bialkowska

If you are still considering whether or not this is the right dog for you, think about how easily you are frustrated when kids and animals don't listen to you. If you have a hard time dealing with disobedience, this is probably not the right dog for you. You will learn during housetraining just how easy it is for a Shiba to learn when he wants to, which may make you think that teaching other commands will be easy. Unfortunately, this is not the case. If he doesn't want to do something, your Shiba Inu will ignore you. For example, while your Shiba Inu will understand the command to sit, he'll only obey if it suits him.

Shiba take a considerable amount of work, and while they are definitely worth the time and effort, people new to taking care of dogs are less likely to be successful. This can lead to families returning their pups. When people talk about herding cats, that expression could just as easily be herding Shiba Inu. They are an incredibly difficult dog to train, which is made all the more frustrating because you know they can learn, they just don't want to. It takes a lot of work in the beginning and a very firm and consistent approach to training. For some, even that won't be enough because they are simply too independent to do tricks.

*Photo Courtesy of
Trisha Cutright*

CHAPTER 3
Finding Your Shiba Inu

If you think that you can give a Shiba Inu the right love and guidance, then you need to make sure you find the right breeder or know the right questions to ask if you want a full-grown dog.

Adult vs Puppy

That will be your next big decision – how much work can you manage? Will you be able to deal with an excitable puppy that has everything to learn? Or do you prefer to work with an adult that may have problems that you have to help the dog work through? Puppies are almost always more work, but you never know what kind of experience an adult dog has been through which will affect how he reacts to the world around him.

The hunt to find your newest family member is going to take a while, even if you decide to rescue an adult. Even though Shiba Inu are fairly healthy, there are some problems that can result from improper breeding and care at the beginning of a Shiba Inu's life. To ensure that you get a healthy puppy that will be your loving companion for as long as possible, you have to find a reputable breeder who cares more about the puppies than the money.

Photo Courtesy of
Rachel Deihl

Considerations And Steps To Rescue An Adult Shiba Inu

The approach to adopting an adult Shiba Inu is the same as it is for adopting a puppy from a breeder. However, with such an intelligent, independent dog, you are going to want to ask a lot more questions about adopting an adult, particularly about the dog's previous experiences.

Considerations

Rescuing any dog comes with some inherent risks. While it is possible to find Shiba Inu puppies at dog rescues, it is much more likely that you will find a rescued adult. Adopting an older Shiba Inu could require a lot of work, and their history is incredibly important so you know what to expect.

FUN FACT
Puppy Cam

In October 2008, a litter of Shiba Inu puppies was born in San Francisco. What's unique about this litter is that their early days were recorded and broadcast on a livestream for the world to enjoy. This litter of puppies quickly became an internet sensation. The six puppies' names were Autumn, Ayumi, Amaya, Aki, Akoni, and Ando. They soon became known as "the Shiba Six." The dogs' owners remain anonymous but have used this litter's fame as an opportunity to fundraise for Shiba Inu rescue organizations. A further six litters have been born, and as of 2013, the puppy cam has raised an estimated $30,000 for charity.

Since they can be very stubborn, people may give up on a Shiba without putting much effort into it. If a dog has not been properly socialized it can be tricky to bring him into a home with other pets. They usually aren't too much of a risk, but they may bother your cats and other small animals.

As with any adult dog, there are some considerations you need to really think about before you decide to adopt another dog. With a breed like the Shiba Inu, you need to consider your current situation and your level of patience, as well as what it is you want from your new canine companion. There is good reason why Shiba Inu are compared to cats, which will not make them great if you want a dog that follows you around and listens to your every word.

Think about the following to determine if an adult Shiba Inu is a good fit for your home.

1. **Why do you want to bring an adult into your home? What are you expectations for the dog?**

   Shiba Inu are adorable, but they are very independent. They may understand the commands you are giving, but simply are not in the mood to do what you tell them. Perhaps it is better to think of them

Photo Courtesy of
Vasiliki Georgopoulos

as small teenagers because they have their own way of thinking and know what they want. If this doesn't align with what you are asking of them, there is a good chance that they won't follow your commands.

2. Do you have the patience to work through the issues that an adult may have?

Rescue organizations collect as much information as they can about the dogs they rescue, but their knowledge of a dog's history is usually very limited. The benefits of rescuing a Shiba Inu are very similar to adopting any rescue dog, but if they are not properly trained you may have some work ahead of you. You need to know about their temperament so you can start planning how to help the dog to overcome past experiences and how to resolve the issues. The odds are very good that you aren't going to be starting from scratch with housetraining. Adult dogs are awake more often than puppies and, while it may take them a bit longer to warm up to you, you can bond much faster with an adult, depending on their age. Adult Shiba Inu may be a bit more wary, especially if they were not socialized or were previously treated poorly, but that loving disposition will likely come out fairly quickly once they start to feel safe and at home. Your new dog may not to want to cuddle with you in the early days either (and may not ever become fond of it), which may be a bit dispiriting, but give the dog time and you may be able to convince him to be a bit more sociable. Once your adult dog bonds with you, it will be like flipping an affection switch, and then you really could not ask for a more loving, loyal, and intelligent canine.

3. Are you able to properly dog proof your home before the dog arrives?

You can't simply bring an adult dog into your home and let him run around unchecked. One thing that is similar to preparing your home for puppies is that you will want to dog proof your home for a rescue. You will need to have everything set up before the dog arrives. Most people think it isn't necessary to prepare for an adult dog and fail to properly get their home ready, a huge mistake when you bring home such an adept escape artist. Like a puppy, you will need to have a dedicated space for your new dog to make sure he learns the rules before being allowed to roam the home. They can be very destructive when they are bored, so you do not want your dog being free without knowing the house rules. That said, you should not keep a Shiba Inu adult locked up in a crate the majority of the time. In the beginning you will need a large space for the dog to get familiar with you and your home as you assess your new dog's personality and capabilities. It is a fairly important consideration, particularly if you have other dogs and cats, as you will want to ensure harmony in your home.

4. **Do you have pets who will be affected by the introduction of an alpha dog?**

Shiba Inu are not intimidated by larger dogs or animals. To them, anyone and everyone is a potential minion. They want to be in charge, and so your first job is to make sure your puppy learns that he is not the boss. This can be very disruptive in homes with an alpha dog already present. Your cats may or may not be bothered by the introduction of a Shiba Inu. Chapter 8 covers how Shiba Inu will likely affect different pets, but you need to think about this before you decide to introduce a Shiba Inu into your home.

Good Shiba Inu-specific rescue organizations are cautious about adopting out a rescue with personality and socialization issues (there are some, including dogs from puppy mills and those that had negligent or abusive owners before being rescued). Rescue shelters will be less careful about adopting out Shiba Inu because they are popular and low risk to most homes.

You may not be able to get a complete health record for an adult Shiba Inu, but it is likely that you will find a dog that has already been spayed or neutered, as well as chipped. Unless you adopt a Shiba Inu that has health issues (these should be disclosed by the rescue organization if available), rescues tend to be less costly at the first vet visit than puppies – for the first few years it's likely you won't pay nearly as much to take care of your Shiba Inu's health. You will be spending a lot more time training and exercising though. Puppies have a short attention span, which equates to many short training sessions. Adults require more attention and long durations of training so that they get accustomed to listening to you. This dedicated attention is good not only for teaching the rules of the home, but for bonding with the dog.

Older dogs give you more immediate gratification. You don't have to go through those sleepless nights with a new puppy or the endless frustration that comes with the early types of training. All intelligent dogs require a lot of the same time and attention as puppies. Bypassing that is a major part of the appeal of older dogs. However, you do have to be much more cautious as they will likely take longer to get acclimated to their new home.

Finally, one of the biggest benefits of getting an adult (besides getting to skip housetraining) – they are already their full size. You don't have to guess or estimate the size your dog will be, making it far easier to get the right gear and dog supplies in the beginning.

The following are some Shiba Inu rescue organizations to help you get started:

- Shiba Inu Rescue Association
- National Shiba Inu Rescue
- My First Shiba – List of Rescue Organizations – provides a number of regional rescues so you can find a place close to you.

Don't forget that breeders may also have older dogs that they are willing to adopt out to a loving family. Contracts and guarantees are meant as much to protect the puppies, as the families who adopt them. If you want an adult, consider calling breeders to see if they have any adults available. You will need to ask them a different set of questions than if you were adopting a puppy, but they will be able to provide you with a lot of details about the dog, his personality, and if there are any potential issues.

Steps to Rescuing a Shiba Inu

If you are interested in looking into adopting from a rescue organization or group, there are several things to keep in mind. This section covers the questions you should ask. If you are considering adopting a puppy from a rescue group instead of a breeder, ask the same questions provided in that section to know what questions to ask before adopting a puppy.

If you look to a breeder to adopt an adult, you can use this section to question them as well.

To get a better idea of the rescue organization and how much they know about the dogs they adopt out, ask the following questions.

- What was the reason the dog was surrendered?
- Did the dog have any health issues when he arrived?
- Do they know how the dog was treated by the previous family (including what kind of training the dog has had, if he was mistreated, or if he was socialized)?
- How many homes do they know the dog has been in?
- What kind of vet care has the dog had? Do they have records from before the dog arrived into their care?
- Will the dog require extra medical attention based on known or suspected problems?

- Is the dog housetrained?
- How well does the dog react to strangers and walks in familiar areas?
- Does the dog walk well on a leash, or will a special halter (such as a gentle lead or harness) be required?
- Does the dog have good eating habits? Does he tend to be more aggressive when eating?
- How does the dog react to children and other pets?
- Does the dog have any known additional dietary restrictions?
- Will the organization take the dog back if there are problems identified with the dog after adoption?

Breeders can be a great source for adopting older Shiba Inu, particularly if you already have pets in the home. Since the adult dog is currently living with other dogs, it means that they have a certain level of socialization and may already know how to keep from trying to be the boss from the beginning. The breeders also have a more complete knowledge of the Shiba Inu's history, which is always preferable for pure breeds.

Considerations For Adopting A Puppy And Picking A Breeder

Puppies are a major time investment, and a dog as intelligent and willful as the Shiba Inu will make some aspects of raising a puppy that much harder. There are some considerations you need to really think about before you decide to adopt a puppy.

Think about the following to determine if a Shiba Inu puppy is a good fit for your home.

1. **How much time do you have available? Are you willing to give up all of your free time and work your schedule around your puppy?**

   One of the biggest considerations is how much time are you willing to invest. All puppies are a lot of work, starting with the moment the puppy enters your care. While the breed's temperament is largely predictable, how you train and socialize your puppy will affect nearly every aspect of the dog's adult life. Training and socializing can take up a large chunk of time in the early days, but they are absolutely essential for raising a healthy Shiba Inu.

   You also want the puppy to know that your home is safe and that everyone has the puppy's best interest in mind. This can be exhausting because the dogs have a lot of energy from an early age.

Without proper training and socialization, you may have a dog that is too rambunctious, destructive, and disregarding of your attempts to train him.

2. **Are you able to be firm and consistent with such an adorable puppy?**

From the very beginning, you have to establish yourself and your family as the ones in charge so that your Shiba Inu understands the hierarchy from the moment he enters your home. He may not always listen, but you cannot let him think that he is in charge.

3. **Do you have the time, energy, and budget to puppy proof your home?**

The work to prepare your home for your puppy's arrival begins long before your puppy arrives though. Puppy proofing the home is as time-consuming as childproofing your home. It is essential to puppy proof your home, but you still have to keep a constant eye on your puppy after the little guy arrives. If you do not have the time to puppy proof your home, then you should consider getting an adult dog (you should probably also consider a different breed because a Shiba Inu of any age brought into the home is going to be a large time investment). Chapter 5 provides details about what you need to do to prepare your home.

On the plus side, you will have more time to live together with a puppy than with an adult. You will have records about the puppy and the puppy's parents, making it easier to identify the potential problems your Shiba Inu may suffer. This makes it considerably easier to ensure your puppy stays healthy and catch potential issues earlier.

Some people find it easier to bond with puppies than with adult dogs. A young puppy is going to be nervous in a new home, but most of them adjust quickly because they are predisposed to enjoying the company of those around them. Your primary job will be protecting your puppy and making sure that you patiently train him. We will cover this more in a later chapter.

Finding a responsible breeder is the best thing you can do for your puppy since good breeders work with only healthy parents, reducing the odds that a puppy will have serious health issues. Always take the time to research breeders. Even though this is a breed that is higher maintenance – or at least they require a lot of patience and willingness to work through the stubbornness – most people who are not willing to put time into it won't. Although breeders for Shiba Inu are largely reputable, that doesn't mean there won't be some who are more interested in earning a lot of money.

Choosing A Breeder

Once you understand enough about the breed to know what you are getting into, it is time to start talking to breeders. The goal is to determine which breeders are willing to take the time to patiently and thoroughly answer all of your questions. They should have as much love for their Shiba Inu as they want you to feel for your new puppy. And they should want to make sure that their puppies go to good homes.

If you find someone who posts regular pictures and information about the parents and the progress of the mother's pregnancy and vet visits, that is a very good sign. The best breeders will not only talk about their dogs and the plans for the parents in the future, they will stay in contact with you after you take the puppy home and answer any questions as they arise. These are the kinds of breeders who are likely to have waiting lists. The active interest in knowing about what happens to the puppies later shows that they care a great deal about each individual dog. You also want to find a breeder who is willing to talk about the potential problems with Shiba Inu. Good breeders will want to ensure the family adopting one of their puppies is capable of properly socializing and training a Shiba Inu. Both of these activities are essential as a puppy matures.

It is likely that for each breeder you call the conversation will last about an hour. If a breeder does not have time to talk and isn't willing to talk with you later, you can cross them off your list. After you have talked with each possible breeder, compare answers.

The following are some questions to ask. Make sure you take careful notes while interviewing the breeders:

- Ask if you can visit in person. The answer should always be yes, and if it isn't, you don't need to ask anything further. Thank the breeder and hang up. Even if the breeder is located in a different state, they should allow you to visit the facility.

- Ask about the required health tests and certifications they have for their puppies. These points are detailed further in the next section, so make sure to check off the available tests and certifications for each breeder. If they don't have all of the tests and certifications, you may want to remove the breeder from consideration.

- Make sure that the breeder always takes care of all of the initial health requirements in the first few weeks through the early months, particularly shots. Puppies require that certain procedures be done before they leave their mother to ensure they are healthy. Vaccinations and worming typically start around six weeks after the puppies are born, then need to be continued every three weeks. By the time your puppy is old enough to come home, he should be well into the procedures, or even completely through with the first phases of these important health care needs.

- Ask if the puppy is required to be spayed or neutered before reaching a certain age of maturity. Typically, these procedures are done in the puppies' best interest.

- Find out if the breeder is part of a Shiba Inu organization or group.

- Ask about the first phases of your puppy's life, such as how the breeder plans to care for the puppy during those first few months. They should be able to provide a lot of detail, and they should do this without sounding as though they are irritated that you want to know. They will also let you know how much training you can expect to be done prior to the puppy's arrival in your home. It is possible that the breeder may start housetraining the puppy. Ask how quickly the puppy has picked up on the training. You want to be able to pick up from where the breeder left off once your Shiba Inu reaches your home.

- See what kind of advice the breeder gives about raising your Shiba Inu puppy. They should be more than happy to help guide you to doing what is best for your dog because they will want the puppies to live happy, healthy lives. You should also be able to rely on a breeder's recommendations, advice, and additional care after the puppy arrives at your home. Basically, you are getting customer support, as well as a great chance of having a healthy dog.

- How many breeds do they manage a year? How many sets of parents do the breeders have? Puppies can take a lot of time and attention, and the mother should have some downtime between pregnancies. Learn about the breeder's standard operations to find out if they are taking care of the parents and treating them like valuable family members and not strictly as a way to make money.

- Ask about aggression in the parents. Also find out if they have other dog breeds in the home. While puppies are more temperamentally malleable than adults, if they have already had some exposure to other breeds, it may make it easier to integrate them into a home that already has dogs.

Contracts And Guarantees

Breeder contracts and guarantees are meant to protect the puppies as much as they are meant to protect you. If a breeder has a contract that must be signed, make sure that you read through it completely and are willing to meet all of the requirements prior to signing it. The contracts tend to be fairly easy to understand and comply with, but you should be aware of all the facts before you agree to anything. Beyond putting down the money for the puppy, signing the contract says that you are serious about how you plan to take care of the puppy to the best of your abilities by meeting the minimum requirements set forth by the breeder. A contract may also say that the breeder will retain the puppy's original registration papers, although you can get a copy of the papers.

When a family does not live up to the agreement from the contract, the breeder is able to take the puppy away from that family. These are the dogs that some breeders have available for adoption.

The guarantee states what health conditions the breeder promises for their puppies. This typically includes details about the dog's health and recommendations on the next steps of the puppy's care once it leaves the breeder's facility. Guarantees may also provide schedules to ensure that the health care started by the breeder is continued by the new puppy parent. In the event that a major health concern is found, the puppy will need to be returned to the breeder. The contract will also explain what is not guaranteed. The guarantee tends to be very long (sometimes longer than the contract), and you should read it thoroughly before you sign it.

Shiba Inu contracts usually come with a requirement to have the dog spayed or neutered once it reaches maturity (typically six months). The contract may also contain naming requirements, health details, and a stipulation for what will happen if you can no longer take care of the animal (the dog usually goes back to the breeder). It could also include information on what will happen if you are negligent or abusive to your dog.

Photo Courtesy of Brooke Steinbach

Health Tests And Certifications

"It is important to know where your Shiba pup is coming from. A breeder should allow you to see the parent's history. If they do not wish to share that with you, then I would pick another breeder who will. Hip dysplasia is something to look for, eyes, bite, stance, the point and curve of the ears and more."

Jan Hill
Dark Knight Shibas

A healthy puppy requires healthy parents and a clean genetic history. A good breeder keeps extensive records of each puppy and the parents. You will want to review each of the parents' complete history to understand what traits your puppy is likely to inherit. Pay attention to learning abilities, temperament, clinginess, and any personality trait you consider important. You can either request that documents be sent electronically to you or get them when you visit the breeder in person.

It could take a while to review the breeder's information about each parent, but it is always well worth the time you spend studying and planning. The more you know about the parents, the better prepared you will be for your puppy.

When looking for a Shiba Inu to adopt, there are a few health concerns that you should ask breeders or rescue groups about.

The following are health tests all breeders should ensure their Shiba Inu undergo:

- Hip and elbow evaluation – testing the puppies for dysplasia
- Patella evaluation – an issue with a dog's kneecaps
- Eye examination by someone who is a member of the ACVO Ophthalmologist (they should be registered with either the OFA or the CERF)

Breeders who take the time to join the National Shiba Club of America prove that they are serious about the health of their puppies. This organization requires that a standardized set of requirements be met, so membership denotes that the breeders who join are reliable and reputable.

Selecting A Puppy From A Breeder

"The Shiba pup that comes right up to you is likely to be more of a 'test the limits' type dog. Shy is not necessarily good though because a shy Shiba can get nippy if cornered. Watch alertness and high tails: those are signs of dominance. That can be good if that is what you want but make sure you know that the more dominance a pup show the more likely it will be to test its limits and push to see how far you will allow it to go."

Jeffrey Kellen
JAK Kennel

Selecting your puppy should be done in person. However, you can start checking out your puppy after birth if the breeder is willing to share videos and pictures. When you are finally allowed to see the puppies in person, consider the following:

- Assess the group of puppies as a whole. If most or all of the puppies are aggressive or fearful, this is an indication of a problem with the litter or (more likely) the breeder. Here are a few red flags if displayed by a majority of the puppies:
    - Tucked tails
    - Shrinking away from people
    - Whimpering when people get close
    - Constant attacking of your hands or feet (beyond pouncing)
- Notice how well each puppy plays with the others. This is a great indicator of just how well your puppy will react to any pets you already have at home.
- Notice which puppies greet you first, and which ones hang back to observe.
- The puppies should not be fat or underweight, which admittedly, can be difficult to tell with their thick coats. A swollen stomach is generally a sign of worms or other health problems.
- Puppies should have straight, sturdy legs. Splayed legs can be a sign that there is something wrong.
- Examine the puppy's ears for mites, which will cause discharge. The inside of the ear should be pink, not red or inflamed.

- The eyes should be clear and bright.
- Check the puppy's mouth for pink, healthy-looking gums.
- Pet the puppy to check his coat for the following:
  - Ensure that the coat feels thick and full. If the breeder has allowed the fur to get matted or really dirty, it is an indication that they likely are not taking proper care of the animals.
  - Check for fleas and mites by running your hand from the head to the tail, then under the tail (fleas are more likely to hide under most dogs' tails). Mites may look like dandruff.
- Check the puppy's rump for redness and sores and see if you can check the last bowel movement to ensure it is firm.

Pick the puppy that exhibits the personality traits that you want in your dog. If you want a forward, friendly, excitable dog, the first puppy to greet you may be the one you seek. If you want a dog that will think things through and let others get more attention, look for a puppy that sits back and observes you before approaching.

Photo Courtesy of
Janice Hill
Darknight Shibas

CHAPTER 4
Preparing Your Family

Preparing your family and pets for a Shiba Inu will probably intensify the excitement as you prepare for this foxlike love to arrive. Initially, there will be some question of who is in charge, and this can be very frustrating. You will need to not only remember this yourself, you will want to make sure all of the members of your family keep this in mind. That is just one of the first rules that you must make sure is in place before your Shiba Inu arrives.

Planning The First Year's Budget

FUN FACT
Bodhi the Stylish Pup

Bodhi is undoubtedly the most fashionable dog on the internet with a style his owner, Yena Kim, describes as "classic with a touch of vintage and a touch of trend." This trendy Shiba Inu rose to fame on Instagram when Kim decided to dress him up in a shirt to see how he would react. Supposedly Bodhi immediately took to modeling and life has never been the same. Bodhi, now known as the Menswear Dog, has appeared in numerous magazine spreads and has published a book, *Menswear Dog Presents the New Classics: Fresh Looks for the Modern Man.*

Caring for a puppy is a lot more expensive than you would think. You will need to have a budget, which is a good reason to start purchasing supplies a few months in advance. When you buy the items you need, you will begin to see exactly how much you will spend a month. Of course there are some items that are one-time purchases, but many other items will need to be purchased regularly, like food and treats.

Begin budgeting the day you decide to get your puppy. The cost will include the adoption fee, which is typically higher for a purebred dog than for a rescue dog.

The vet and other healthcare costs, such as regular vaccinations and an annual checkup, should be included in your budget.

The following table can help you start to plan your budget. Keep in mind that the prices are a rough averages, and may be significantly different based on where you live.

Item	Considerations	Estimated Costs
Crate	This should be a comfortable space where the puppy will sleep and rest.	Wire crates: Range $60 to $350 Portable crate: Range $35 to $200
Bed	This will be placed in the crate.	$10 to $55
Leash	It should be short in the beginning because you need to be able to keep your puppy from getting overexcited and running to the end of a long line.	Short leash: $6 to $15 Retractable: $8 to $25
Doggie bags for walks	If you walk at parks, this won't be necessary. For those who don't have daily access to bags, it is best to purchase packs to ensure you don't run out of bags.	Singles cost less than $1 each. Packs: $4 to $16
Collar	This should fit comfortably without being too loose or tight. It can be difficult to get it right at first, and you will need to adjust it as your puppy grows.	$10 to $30
Tags	These will likely be provided by your vet. Find out what information the vet provides on tags, then purchase any tags that are not provided. At a minimum, your Shiba Inu should have tags with your address on it in case the pup escapes.	Contact your vet before purchasing to see if the required rabies tags include your contact info.
Puppy food	This will depend on if you make your Shiba Inu food, if you purchase food, or both. The larger the bag, the higher the cost, but the fewer times you will need to purchase food. You will need to purchase puppy specific food in the beginning, but will stop after the second year. Adult dog food is more expensive, so you will need to plan for an increase in cost once your puppy reaches adulthood.	$9 to $90 per bag
Water and food bowls	These will need to be kept in the puppy's designated area. If you have other dogs, you will need separate food bowls for the puppy. If your puppy proves to be an avid chewer, consider getting a stainless steel bowl.	$10 to $40

Toothbrush/ Toothpaste	You will need to brush his teeth regularly, so plan to buy more than one toothbrush during the first year.	$2.50 t0 $14
Brush	Shiba Inu coats are fairly easy to maintain, but you should still brush them regularly. When they are puppies, brushing offers a great way to bond.	$3.50 to $20
Toys	You definitely want to get your puppy toys, and you are going to want toys for more aggressive chewers, even if your puppy goes through them remarkably quickly. You may want to keep getting your Shiba Inu toys as an adult (cost of adult dog toys not included).	$2.00 Packs of toys range from $10 to $20 (easier in the long run as your pup will chew through toys quickly)
Training treats	You will need these from the beginning, and likely won't need to change the treats based on your Shiba Inu's age; you may need to change treats to keep your dog's interest though.	$4.50 to $15

The difference between the puppy and an adult in size is not substantial, so you won't need to get two different crates or other supplies. However, you will need to adjust some of the pet supplies, such as the collar.

Instructing Children

You want your pup to feel comfortable from the start, which means making sure your children are careful and gentle with the dog, whether you're planning on adopting a puppy or an adult. This is a breed that looks absolutely adorable, and some kids may try to treat them like a toy or stuffed animal, which could be detrimental to your dog – especially if you get a puppy. You will need to make sure your kids follow all of the rules from the beginning to ensure that your puppy feels safe and happy in your home.

Refresh the following rules regularly, both before the puppy arrives and after the arrival. Older teens will probably be all right to help with the puppy, but younger teens and kids should not be left alone with the puppy for a few months. Remember that you will need to be very firm to make sure that the puppy is not hurt or frightened.

The following are the five golden rules that your children should follow from the very first interaction.

Photo Courtesy of
Pervie Villareal

1. Always be gentle and respectful.
2. Do not disturb the puppy during mealtime.
3. Chase is an outside game.
4. Don't play tug until the puppy is trained.
5. The Shiba Inu should always remain firmly on the ground.
6. All of your valuables should be kept well out of the puppy's reach.

Since your kids are going to ask why, here are the explanations you can give them. You can simplify them for younger kids, or start a dialogue with teens.

Always Be Gentle And Respectful

Little Shiba Inu puppies are very cute and cuddly, but they are also more fragile than their rugged appearance suggests. At no time should anyone play rough with the puppy (or any adult Shiba Inu). It is important to be respectful of your puppy to help that puppy learn to also be respectful toward people and other animals.

This rule must be applied consistently every time your children play with the puppy. Be firm if you see your children getting too excited or rough. You don't want the puppy to get overly excited either because he might end up nipping or biting someone. If he does, it isn't his fault because he hasn't learned better yet – it is the child's fault. Make sure your children understand the possible repercussions if they get too rough.

Mealtime

Shiba Inu, like nearly every breed, can be protective of their food, especially if you rescue a dog that has previously had to fend for himself. Even if you have a puppy, you don't want him to feel insecure about his food because that will teach him to be aggressive when he is eating, which is obviously not fair to your Shiba Inu. Save yourself, your family, and your Shiba Inu trouble by making sure everyone knows that eating time is your Shiba Inu's time alone. Similarly, teach your kids that their own mealtime is off limits to the puppy. No feeding him from the table.

Photo Courtesy of
Inger Lise Fløtten

Chase

Make sure your kids understand why a game of chase is fine outside (though you'll need to monitor it), but inside the house the game is off limits.

Running inside the home gives your Shiba Inu puppy the impression that your home isn't safe inside because he is being chased. And it teaches your puppy that running indoors is fine, which can be very dangerous as the dog gets older and bigger. One of the last things you want is for your Shiba Inu to go barreling through your home knocking people off their feet because it was fine for him to run in the house when he was a puppy.

Tug

Tug is a game that should always wait until puppies of any breed are trained to listen to you. From toys to blankets to pillows, your puppy is going to want to play tug. But first, you have to establish what is and isn't a game. Don't send mixed signals to the puppy. If you play the game too early, it will encourage your dog to challenge you. With a stubborn breed like the Shiba Inu, you don't want to give the puppy the wrong idea. It's best to wait until the dog has been properly trained before engaging in this particular game.

Paws On The Ground

This is a rule that will likely require a good bit of explaining to your children as Shiba Inu look a lot like toys, especially Shiba Inu puppies. No one should be picking the puppy up off the ground. You may want to carry your new family member around or play with the pup like a baby, but you and your family will need to resist that urge. Kids particularly have trouble understanding since they will see the Shiba Inu puppy more like a toy than a living creature. The younger your children are, the more difficult it will be for them to understand the difference. It is so tempting to treat the Shiba Inu like a baby and to try to carry him like one, but this is incredibly uncomfortable and unhealthy for the puppy. Older kids will quickly learn that a puppy's nip or bite hurts a lot more than you would think. Those little teeth are quite sharp, and you don't want the puppy to be dropped. If your children learn never to pick up the puppy things will go a lot better. Remember, this also applies to you, so don't make things difficult by doing something you constantly tell your children not to do.

Photo Courtesy of
Brooke Steinbach

Keep Valuables Out Of Reach

Valuables are not something you want to end up in the puppy's mouth, whether it's toys, jewelry, or shoes. Your kids will be less than happy if their personal possessions are chewed up by an inquisitive puppy, so teach them to put toys, clothes, and other valuables far out of the puppy's reach.

Preparing Your Current Dogs

Shiba Inu tend to be domineering. When they are puppies, you have a chance to start socializing them with your other dogs so that they know the hierarchy as early as possible. You don't need to establish the hierarchy, but you do need to make sure everyone is comfortable and certain of where they are in the pack. This means if you already have canines in your home, they are going to need to be prepared for the new arrival.

Here are the important tasks to do to prepare your current pets for your new arrival.

- Set a schedule for the activities you will need to do and the people who will need to participate.
- Preserve your current dogs' favorite places and furniture, and make sure their toys and items are not in the puppy's space.
- Have playdates at your home and analyze your dogs to see how they react to an addition.

Photo Courtesy of Karolina Bialkowska

Stick To A Schedule

Photo Courtesy of Sophie Riggs

Obviously, the puppy is going to get a lot of attention, so you need to make a concerted effort to let your current canine know that you still love and care for him. Make a specific time in your schedule just for your current dog or dogs, and make sure that you don't stray from that schedule after the puppy's arrival.

Make sure that you plan to have at least one adult around for each other dog you have. Cats are generally less of a concern, but you will probably want to have at least one other adult around when the puppy comes home. We will go into more detail later about what the roles of the other adults will be, but, for now, when you know what date you will be bringing your puppy home, ensure that you have additional adults to help out. You may need to remind them as the time nears, so set an alert on your phone, as well as the date, time, and pickup information for your puppy.

One benefit of having a schedule for your other dogs in place before your Shiba Inu puppy arrives is that it will then be easy to keep a schedule with the puppy. Shiba Inu love to know what to expect, at least in the beginning. This may change as they age, as this breed does like to have a good bit of independence, like a cat.

Your puppy is going to eat, sleep, and spend most of the day and night in his assigned space. This means that the space cannot block your current canine from his favorite furniture, bed, or any place where he rests over the course of the day. None of your current dog's stuff should be in this area, and this includes toys. You don't want your dog to feel like the puppy is taking over his territory. Make sure your children understand to never to put your current dog's stuff in the puppy's area.

Your dog and the puppy will need to be kept apart in the early days, (even if they seem friendly) until your puppy is done with vaccinations. Puppies are more susceptible to illness during these days, so wait until the puppy is protected before the dogs spend time together. Leaving the puppy in the puppy space will keep them separated during this critical time.

Helping Your Dog Prepare – Extra At Home Playdates

Here are things that will best help prepare your pooch for the arrival of your puppy.

- Think about your dog's personality to help you decide the best way to prepare for that first day, week, and month. Each dog is unique, so you will need to consider your dog's personality to determine how things will go when the new dog arrives. If your current dog loves other dogs, this will probably hold true when the puppy shows up. If your dog has any territorial tendencies, you will need to be cautious about the introduction and first couple of months so that your current dog learns that the Shiba Inu is now a part of the pack. Excitable dogs will need special attention to keep them from getting overly agitated when a new dog comes home. You don't want them to be so excited they accidentally hurt the little Shiba Inu.

- Consider the times when you have had other dogs in your home and how your current dog reacted to these other furry visitors. If your canine displayed territorial tendencies, you should be extra careful with how you introduce your new pup. If you haven't ever invited another dog to your home, have a couple of playdates with other dogs at your home before your new Shiba Inu puppy arrives. You have to know how your current furry babies will react to new dogs in the house so you can properly prepare. Meeting a dog at home is very different from encountering one outside the home.

- Think about your dog's interactions with other dogs for as long as you have known the pup. Has your dog shown either protective or possessive behavior, either with you or others? Food is one of the reasons dogs will display some kind of aggression because they don't want anyone trying to eat what is theirs. Some dogs can be protective of people and toys too.

The same rules apply, no matter how many dogs you have. Think about the personalities of all of them as individuals, as well as how they interact together. Just like people, you may find that when they are together your dogs act differently, which you will need to keep in mind as you plan their first introduction.

See Chapter 8 for planning to introduce your current dogs and your new puppy, and how to juggle a new puppy and your current pets.

Fine With Cats, But Not To Be Trusted With Other Small Animals

"Shibas are NOT recommended for homes with pet rabbits, gerbils, hamsters, birds, etc - they have a very strong prey drive."

Susan Norris-Jones
SunJo Shiba Inu & Japanese Chin

Shiba Inu are incredibly intelligent, which means that they can learn who is a member of the family and who isn't. Since cats clearly have a place in the family (most Shiba Inu will pick this up quickly), your primary concern will be in making sure that your Shiba Inu and cats get along. They all want to be independent, but Shiba Inu also wants to be the boss. There may be some spats early, but most Shiba Inu are not very interested in chasing cats.

Other kinds of pets can be risky with a Shiba Inu. This is a dog that is clever and has thousands of years of training in hunting small animals. The instinct is not quite as honed today, so pets like birds and fish aren't at any real risk. Some of the more exotic types of pets, like rodents and ferrets, may be a source of extreme interest for your Shiba Inu in the early days. It shouldn't take too long for your new dog to learn to ignore them. Going outside on walks could be a different matter though. Squirrels and other small animals running free outside are likely to at least attract your Shiba Inu's attention, if not excite a desire to chase.

CHAPTER 5
Preparing Your Home

"They live to bolt out the front door and can run very fast. Be sure to keep an eye out for them when the front door is opened."

Vicki DeBerry
DeBerry Shiba Inu

Shiba Inu puppies are so very cute because they look like energetic little fluff balls. This can lull people into a false sense of security because they don't realize just how much trouble those adorable little puppies can get into, especially if the new home is not properly prepared for the puppy. Since the dogs are quite small as puppies, owners need to be very careful to make sure to secure everything that the puppy could get into, such as cabinets. As an incredibly intelligent dog, your Shiba Inu

Photo Courtesy of
Brooke Steinbach

Photo Courtesy of
Jerry Simek

is going to be curious and try to get into cabinets, low trash cans and other items around your home that will be easy for him to figure out. Preparing your home both for a puppy small enough to get into tight spaces – especially ones that you think are closed – is a unique challenge that parents of Shiba Inu face. This means taking time to prepare your home before the puppy's arrival.

The week before your puppy arrives, you should conduct numerous checks to ensure that your home is safe for the new family member. Making sure your new Shiba Inu has a safe space with all of the essentials (including toys) will make the arrival of your newest family addition a great time for everyone – especially your new canine companion.

Even if you bring an adult Shiba Inu home, you have to prepare for the arrival of an incredibly headstrong toddler that can get into places that you had not considered possible. Shiba Inu have to learn that you are in control, which means that you have to gain their respect before they will listen to you, and even then they may not always listen if they aren't in the mood. If your dog has not already learned not to grab food, climb on furniture, or whatever other restrictions you have implemented in your home, you will have your work cut out for you when it comes to training your new friend. Dog-proofing your home will help you keep your dog safe while he is learning to listen to you.

Creating A Safe Space For Your Dog Or Puppy

Your puppy is going to need a dedicated space that includes a crate (more information on this in the next section), food and water bowls, pee pads, and toys. All of these things will need to be in the area where the puppy will be when you are not able to give him dedicated attention. The puppy space should be safe and gated so that the puppy cannot get out, and young children and other dogs cannot get in. It should be a safe space where the puppy can see you going about your usual business and feel comfortable.

Crates And Crate Training

Crate training a Shiba Inu puppy can be easier than training most other breeds because of their intelligence and desire for things to be clean. When they are young, they are more likely to listen to you, as long as you are firm and consistent. This means making sure that the puppy's crate and bedding is already setup before your puppy arrives.

Your Shiba Inu's crate needs to be comfortable. Never treat the crate like it is a prison for your puppy. Your Shiba Inu should never associate

Photo Courtesy of
Aldric Manrique

Photo Courtesy of
Brooke Steinbach

the crate with punishment – it's meant to be a safe haven after overstimulation or when it's time to sleep. Ensure your dog never associates the crate with punishment or negative emotions. The crate should be adjustable so that you can make it a bit larger when your puppy becomes an adult. You can also get your puppy a carrying crate in the early days to make trips to the vet a little easier. This crate won't work when your Shiba Inu is an adult (you can just walk your Shiba into the vet's office as an adult), but the carrying crate has plenty of space for a puppy.

As mentioned in an earlier chapter, you can use the crate to help with housetraining. While they do tend to be easy to housetrain, you may want to have a pee pad in the puppy's area as far from the crate as possible. This will give your puppy a place to go during inclement weather. Make sure to find out from the breeder if the puppy has already begun housetraining. If the puppy is already making progress, you may not want to add the pee pad.

Purchase And Prepare Supplies And Tools

Planning for your puppy's arrival means buying a lot supplies up front. The list is longer than most people realize, so take some time to really think about what you will need based on your home and circumstances. If you start making purchases around the time you identify the

Photo Courtesy of
Caitlin Rubinstein

breeder, you can stretch out your expenses over a longer period of time. This will make it seem a lot less expensive than it actually is. The following are recommended items you should have purchased before bringing your new dog home:

- Crate
- Bed
- Leash
- Doggie bags for walks
- Collar
- Tags
- Puppy food
- Water and food bowls (sharing a water bowl is usually okay, but your puppy needs his or her own food dish if you have multiple dogs)
- Toothbrush/Toothpaste
- Brush
- Toys
- Training treats

Talk to your vet before buying any medications, including flea treatments.

Puppy Proof The House

"Treat your new Shiba like a toddler. Make sure all cords, small items and food are kept clear from them getting into or chewing on."

Jan Hill
Dark Knight Shibas

Preparing for the arrival of a puppy is time consuming, and all of the most dangerous rooms and items in your home will be equally as dangerous to your puppy as they would be to a baby. The biggest difference is that your Shiba Inu is going to be mobile much faster than a child. He will potentially get into dangerous situations almost immediately if you don't eliminate all of the dangers ahead of his arrival in your home. Your pup's intelligence is going to mean you need to puppy proof your home for a toddler because a Shiba Inu can figure out how to get into things just like young children do.

Be aware that puppies will try to eat virtually anything, even if it isn't food. Nothing is safe – not even your furniture. They'll gnaw on wood and metal. Anything within their reach is considered to be fair game. Keep this in mind as you go about puppy proofing your home.

Indoor Hazards And Fixes

This section details the areas inside your home where you should focus your attention. In case of problems, have your vet's number posted on the fridge and in at least one other room in the house. If you set this up before your pup arrives, it will be there if you need it. Even if you program the vet's phone number into your phone, another family member or someone taking care of your Shiba Inu may still need it.

Shiba Inu can get into nearly everything at their height, and they will be exploring a lot when given the opportunity. As intelligent as the breed is, it's best to overestimate what your puppy can do and prepare accordingly. Get low and see each room from your Shiba Inu's perspective. You are almost guaranteed to find at least one thing you missed.

Hazards	Fixes	Time Estimate
Kitchen		
Poisons	Keep in secured, childproof cabinets or on high shelves	30 min
Trash cans	Have a lockable trash can, or keep it in a secured location	10 min
Appliances	Make sure all cords are out of reach	15 min
Human Food	Keep out of reach	Constant (start making it a habit)
Floors		
Slippery surfaces	Put down rugs or special mats designed to stick to the floor	30 min – 1 hour
Training area	Train on non-slip surfaces	Constant
Bathrooms		
Toilet brush	Either have one that locks or keep out of reach	5 min/bathroom
Poisons	Keep in secured, childproof cabinets or on high shelves	15 - 30 min/ bathroom
Toilets	Keep closed Do not use automatic toilet cleaning chemicals	Constant (start making it a habit)
Cabinets	Keep locked with childproof locks	15 - 30 min/ bathroom

Laundry Room		
Clothing	Store clean and dirty clothing off the floor, and out of reach	15 – 30 min
Poisons (bleach, pods/detergent, dryer sheets, and misc. poisons)	Keep in secured, childproofed cabinets or on high shelves	15 min
Around the Home		
Plants	Keep off the floor	45 min – 1 hour
Trash cans	Have a lockable trash can, or keep it in a secured location	30 min
Electrical cords, window blind cords	Hide them or makes sure they are out of reach; pay particular attention to entertainment and computer areas	1.5 hours
Poisons	Check to make sure there aren't any (WD40, window/screen cleaner, carpet cleaner, air fresheners); move all poisons to a centralized, locked location	1 hour
Windows	Check that cords are out of reach in all rooms	1 – 2 hours
Fireplaces	Store cleaning supplies and tools where the puppy can't get into them Cover the fireplace opening with something the puppy can't knock over	10 min/fireplace
Stairs	Cordon off so that your puppy can't try to go up or down them; make sure to test any puppy gates	10 – 15 min
Coffee tables/End tables/ Nightstands	Clear of dangerous objects (e.g., scissors, sewing equipment, pens, and pencils) and all valuables	30 – 45 min

If you have a cat, keep the litter box up off the floor. It needs to be somewhere that your cat can easily get to but your Shiba Inu cannot. Since this involves teaching your cat to use the new area, it's something you should do well in advance of the puppy's arrival. You don't want your cat to undergo too many significant changes all at once. The puppy will be enough of a disruption – if your cat associates the change with the puppy, you may find the feline protesting by refusing to use the litter box.

Outdoor Hazards And Fixes

This section details the things outside your home that need your attention ahead of your puppy's arrival. Also post the vet's number in one of the sheltered areas in case of an emergency.

Hazards	Fixes	Time Estimate
Garage		
Poisons	Keep in secured, childproofed cabinets or on high shelves (e.g., car chemicals, cleaning supplies, paint, lawn care) – this includes fertilizer	1 hour
Trash bins	Keep them in a secured location	5 min
Tools (e.g., lawn, car, hardware, power tools)	Make sure all cords are out of reach: Keep out of reach and never hanging over the side of surfaces	30 min – 1 hour
Equipment (e.g., sports, fishing)	Keep out of reach and never hanging over the side of surfaces	Constant (start making it a habit)
Sharp implements	Keep out of reach and never hanging over the side of surfaces	30 min
Bikes	Store off the ground or in a place the Shiba Inu cannot get to (to keep the pup from biting the tires)	20 min
Fencing (Can Be Done Concurrently)		
Breaks	Fix any breaks in the fencing. Shiba Inu are escape artists, so you need to make sure they can't easily get out of your yard.	30 min - 1 hour
Gaps	Fill any gaps, even if they are intentional, so your Shiba Inu doesn't escape	30 min - 1 hour
Holes/Dips at Base	Fill any area that can be easily crawled under	1 – 2 hours
Yard		
Poisons	Don't leave any poisons in the yard	1 – 2 hours
Plants	Verify that all low plants aren't poisonous to dogs; fence off anything that is (such as grape vines)	45 min – 1 hour
Tools (e.g., lawn maintenance and gardening tools)	Make sure they are out of reach; Make sure nothing is hanging over outdoor tables	30 min – 1 hour

Never leave your Shiba Inu alone in the garage, even when he is an adult. It is likely that your puppy will be in the garage when you take car trips, which is why it is important to puppy proof it. You should always have an eye on the dog, but you obviously can't climb under the car and will have a hard time getting into smaller spaces if your Shiba Inu makes a break for it to explore.

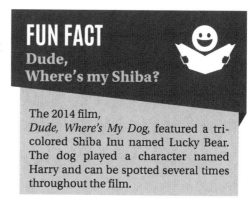

FUN FACT
Dude, Where's my Shiba?

The 2014 film, *Dude, Where's My Dog,* featured a tricolored Shiba Inu named Lucky Bear. The dog played a character named Harry and can be spotted several times throughout the film.

Shiba Inu are escape artists, and they will come up with many new and inventive ways to get out. Do not make it easy for them; take care of all breaks, gaps, and damage to the fence so that your dog can't make any opening big enough to get out of your yard.

Just like with the inside, you will need to follow up your outdoor preparations by getting low and checking out all areas from a puppy's perspective. Again, you are all but guaranteed to find at least one thing you missed.

CHAPTER 6
Planning For Your Shiba Inu's Health

FUN FACT
Mari the Hero

When an earthquake struck the village of Yamakoshi in Japan, a Shiba Inu named Mari rescued not only her three puppies from the rubble, but also alerted her elderly owner in time to escape. Even though her owner was forced to leave Mari and her puppies behind in order to be rescued, upon his return he was delighted to find that the dogs were still alive and safe. The story of Mari's heroism was made into a film in 2007.

Since the breed was brought back from near extinction, a lot more caution has been exercised to ensure that the Shiba Inu doesn't have many genetic illnesses. However, the way you raise your puppy or adult greatly affects his health too. At least one half hour walk is recommended a day, but this is a breed that can exercise for more than an hour if you are an outdoor enthusiast. If you prefer to stay at home and lounge about, a 30 minute walk once a day is fine. Chapters 16 and 17 provide details on genetic issues and general health concerns for any age Shiba Inu.

Choosing Your Veterinarian

Start looking around for a vet for your Shiba Inu even before you choose a breeder. You should have your vet chosen before you bring your dog home. Whether you get a puppy or an adult, you should take your canine to the vet within 48 hours (24 hours is strongly recommended) of his arrival to make sure your dog is healthy. If there is a vet near you who specializes in or has worked with several Shiba Inu before, that will be best for your pup. Considering the Shiba Inu personality, you want a vet who knows how to work with a headstrong pooch. Getting an appointment with a vet can take a while, especially one that specializes in a particular breed, just like getting a doctor's appointment. You need to have your vet and the first appointment booked well in advance of your dog's arrival.

Here are some things to consider when looking for a vet:
- What is the level of familiarity with Shiba Inu? The vet doesn't have to be a specialist, but if you can find someone with some experience

with the canine breed, the vet can help you know what to expect in the different stages of your dog's life. With stubborn, independent breeds like the Shiba Inu, who don't always want to do what they are told, the appointment can take longer. If you can find a vet who knows how to cajole your Shiba Inu into listening, it will be a much better experience for everyone.

Photo Courtesy of
Ashley Antill

Photo Courtesy of
Sandy Li

- How far from your home is the vet? You don't want the vet to be more than 30 minutes away in case of an emergency.
- Is the vet available for emergencies after hours or can they recommend a vet in case of an emergency?
- Is the vet part of a local vet hospital if needed, or does the doctor refer patients to a local pet hospital?
- Is the vet the only vet or one of several partners? If he or she is part of a partnership, can you stick with just one vet for office visits?
- How are appointments booked?
- Can you have other services performed there, such as grooming and boarding?
- Is the vet accredited?
- What are the prices for the initial visit and the normal costs, such as for shots and regular visits?
- What tests and checks are performed during the initial visit?

Make time to visit the vet you are considering so that you can look around to see what the environment is like inside the office. See if you can speak to the vet to see if he or she is willing to help put you at ease and answer your questions. A vet's time is valuable, but he or she should have a few minutes to help you feel confident that he/she is the right choice to help take care of your canine.

Dangerous Foods

Dogs can eat raw meat without having to worry about the kinds of problems a person will encounter. However, there are some human foods that could be fatal to your Shiba Inu. You should keep these foods away from all dogs:

Photo Courtesy of Jamie Joeyen Waldorf

- Apple seeds
- Chocolate
- Coffee
- Cooked bones (they can kill a dog when the bones splinter in the dog's mouth or stomach)
- Corn on the cob (the cob is deadly to dogs; corn off the cob is fine)
- Grapes/raisins
- Macadamia nuts
- Onions and chives
- Peaches, persimmons, and plums
- Tobacco (your Shiba Inu will not know that it is not a food and may eat it if it's left out)
- Xylitol (a sugar substitute in candies and baked goods)
- Yeast

In addition to these potentially deadly foods, there is a long list of things that your dog shouldn't eat. The Canine Journal has a lengthy list of foods (http://www.caninejournal.com/foods-not-to-feed-dog/) that should be avoided.

Photo Courtesy of
Rachel Deihl

A Healthy Dog, With Allergies

Chapter 16 goes into more details about Shiba Inu allergies, but this is definitely a problem you should monitor your Shiba Inu for as he grows. Since this is a breed that has a list of known allergies, you want to make sure to be aware of when your dog is exhibiting allergies. From foods with wheat or chicken to grasses and detergents, Shiba Inu can be allergic to nearly as many things as people. Unlike people, dogs tend to itch when they have allergies, instead of itchy eyes and runny noses, dogs tend to itch all over their bodies. Even though this sounds more symptomatic of rashes, dogs' skin tends to be the way they exhibit most types of allergies, including inhalant allergies. This can make it harder to determine what is wrong, as itching is symptomatic of a lot of possible issues. If you notice your puppy or new Shiba Inu scratching frequently, take him to the vet to see what is wrong, keeping in mind allergies are a potential issue. Fortunately, they are easy to treat, as is covered in a later chapter.

CHAPTER 7
Bringing Your Shiba Inu Home

That first time you walk through the door with your Shiba Inu is a feeling that you will remember years later. Each dog adapts differently, but it is always interesting to see just how this particular breed reacts to a new place. Shiba Inu' natural intelligence will make your puppy more likely to be curious, though if you rescued an adult dog, any exploration will likely be wary. Make sure to read Chapter 8 about how to introduce your adult dog to a multi-pet home. While Shiba Inu don't tend to be aggressive, the first few interactions may be tense as your new dog wants to be the boss.

Final Preparations And Planning

Most intelligent breeds require a constant presence for the first week and as much of the first month as possible. To do this, you may need to take time off from work or negotiate working from home during at least the first 24 hours, if not the first 48 hours. The more time you can dedicate to helping your new friend get accustomed to the new surroundings

Photo Courtesy of
Alayne Levine

Photo Courtesy of
Brooke Steinbach

in those first few days, the better for your new family member and the more quickly he will feel comfortable in his new environment.

The following are some useful checklists to get you through the preparation for your puppy and the aftermath of his arrival at your home.

Ensure You Have Food And Other Supplies On Hand

Do a quick check to ensure that you have everything you need. If you created a list based on the basic supplies from Chapter 5, bring that out the day before your Shiba Inu arrives and make sure you have everything on it. Take a few moments to consider if there is anything you are missing, too. This will hopefully save you from having to try to rush out after the arrival of your new family member.

Design A Tentative Puppy Schedule

Prepare a tentative schedule to help you get started over the course of the week. Your days are about to get very busy, so you need somewhere to start before your puppy arrives. Use the information from Set a Schedule to get started, but make sure you do this earlier instead of later. The following are the three important areas to have established for your puppy's schedule:

- Feeding
- Training (including housetraining)
- Playing

When you bring home a puppy, you may be expecting the high energy that you will see when your Shiba Inu is an adult. However, puppies of any breed (no matter how active they will be later) require a lot of sleep. Expect your puppy to sleep between 18 and 20 hours per day. Having a predictable sleep schedule will help your puppy to grow up healthier.

In the beginning, your Shiba Inu won't be high energy, so you won't need to worry about making sure that he is tired out by the end of the day. His stamina will build fairly quickly, though, so by the end of the first year, your pup will be a lot more active. One of the best things about the breed is that they tend to have energy levels appropriate to their situation, so you aren't going to be as hard pressed to tire your Shiba Inu out as you would a Beagle or Jack Russel Terrier. You will still need to make sure that he gets enough exercise based on his caloric intake, but beyond that, your Shiba Inu will probably adopt an energy level that matches your lifestyle.

In the early days, your puppy's schedule will largely revolve around sleeping and eating, with walking, and socialization. Waking hours will include training and play.

Do A Quick Final Puppy Proofing Inspection Before The Puppy Arrives

No matter how busy you are, or how carefully you followed the puppy proofing checklists from the previous chapter, you still need to take the time to inspect your home one more time before the puppy arrives. Set aside an hour or two to complete this a day or two before the puppy arrives.

Initial Meeting

Have a meeting with all of the family members to make sure all of the rules discussed in Chapter 4 are remembered and understood before the puppy is a distraction. This includes how to handle the puppy. Determine who is going to be responsible for primary puppy care, including who will be the primary trainer. To help teach younger children about responsibility, a parent can pair with a child to manage the puppy's care. The child will be responsible for things like keeping the water bowl filled and feeding the puppy, while a parent oversees the tasks.

Picking Up Your Puppy Or Dog And The Ride Home

FUN FACT
Shiba-San

The Suzuki Tobacco Shop in Japan was well known for its charming shopkeeper, a Shiba Inu! After years of serving his customers, Shiba-san retired in 2015 when the shop closed its doors. Shiba-san drew many customers from around the world to see the four-legged shopkeeper. When he wasn't serving customers, the Shiba Inu could be found lounging in front of the shop's window, chewing his favorite cucumber chew toy.

Picking up your puppy takes a good bit of planning and preparation, especially if you are going to the breeder's home to pick up the puppy. If possible, plan to pick up your puppy on a weekend or at the beginning of a holiday so you can spend unrushed time at home with him. This section covers the preparation and actual trip, but not what to do if you have other dogs that you need to introduce (Chapter 8). If you do not have other dogs, you can pick up your puppy and head straight home. Do not stop anywhere after you have the puppy. If you have a long trip (more than a couple of hours), build breaks into it every few hours to give your puppy a chance to stretch, exercise, drink, and use the bathroom. Do not leave the puppy alone in the car for any amount of time. If you have to use the restroom, at least one adult must remain with the puppy during each stop.

As tempting as it is to cuddle with your puppy and try to make the ride home comfortable, using a crate for the ride home is both safer and more comfortable for the puppy.

Before leaving your home, make sure you have everything you need prepared.

- The crate should be anchored in the car for safety and include a cushion inside the crate. If you have a long trip, bring food and water and plan to stop to give them to the puppy on the trip. Do not put them in the crate as they will not be anchored down, and sloshing water can scare your puppy. You can coat the bottom with a towel or pee pad in case of accidents.

- Call the breeder to make sure everything is still on schedule and make sure the puppy is ready.

- Ask, if you haven't already, if you can get the mother to leave her scent on a blanket to help make the puppy's transition more comfortable.

- Make sure your other adult remembers and will be on time to head to the pick-up destination.
- If you have other dogs, make sure that all of the adults involved know what to do, the time and where to go for that first neutral meeting.

Two adults should be present on the first trip. Ask the breeder if the puppy has been in a car before, and, if not, it is especially important to have someone who can give the puppy attention while the other person drives. The puppy will be in the crate, but someone can still provide comfort. It will definitely be scary because the puppy no longer has mom, siblings, or known people around, so having someone present to talk to the puppy will make it less of an ordeal for the little guy.

This is the time to start teaching your puppy that car trips are enjoyable. This means making sure that the crate is secure. You don't want to terrify the puppy by letting the crate slide around while he is sitting helpless inside it.

When you arrive home, immediately take the puppy or dog outside to use the bathroom. Even if the puppy or dog had an accident on the way, this is the time to start training your new family member where to use the bathroom.

The First Vet Visit And What To Expect

A vet's visit is necessary within the first day or two of your puppy's arrival and may be required in the contract you signed with the breeder. You need to establish a baseline for the puppy's health so that the vet can track your puppy's progress and monitor to ensure everything is going well as your Shiba Inu grows. The initial assessment gives you more information about your puppy, as well as giving you a chance to ask the vet questions and get advice. It also creates an important rapport between your Shiba Inu and the vet.

That first vet visit will be interesting and very different from subsequent visits. Your pup won't know what to expect since he hasn't been to that particular vet before. Try as best as you can to ease his anxiety. You want this first visit to set a positive tone for all future visits.

There are several things that you will need to do before the day of the appointment:

- Find out how early you need to be to complete the paperwork for the new patient.

- Find out if you should bring a stool sample for that first visit, too. If so, collect it the morning of the visit and make sure to take it with you.

- Bring in the paperwork provided by the breeder or rescue organization for the vet to add to your pup's or dog's records.

Upon your arrival, your puppy may want to meet the other pups and people in the office, which is something that can be encouraged as long as you keep some basic rules in mind. After all, this is a chance for you to work on socializing the puppy and to create an initial positive experience to associate with the vet, although you will need to be careful. Always ask the person if it is all right for your puppy to meet any other pet, and wait for approval before letting your puppy move forward with meeting other animals. Pets at the vet's office are very likely to not be feeling great, which means they may not be very affable. You don't want a grumpy older dog or a sick animal to nip or scare your puppy. Negative social experiences are something your puppy will remember, and will make going to the vet something to dread or resist. Nor do you want your puppy to be exposed to potential illnesses while still getting his shots.

During the first visit, the vet will conduct an initial assessment of your Shiba Inu. One of the most important things the vet will do is take your puppy's weight. This is something you are going to have to monitor for your Shiba Inu's entire life because the breed is prone to obesity. Record the weight for yourself so you can see how quickly the puppy is growing. Ask your vet what a healthy weight is at each stage, and record that as well. Shiba Inu grow unbelievably fast during the first year, but you should still make sure your dog isn't gaining more weight than is healthy. During the 2010s, there was a trend of fat Shiba Inu because of how "cute" they looked waddling. This is not only bad for your Shiba Inu's health, it will reduce his life span. To ensure your Shiba Inu stays healthy, you need to know what your dog's weight is upon arrival, then you will have to monitor it over the course of your canine's life to ensure your dog remains healthy.

The vet will set the date for the next set of shots, which will likely happen not too long after your puppy arrives. When it is time for his vaccinations, be prepared for a day or two of your puppy feeling under the weather.

Crate And Other Preliminary Training

"Do not leave them in a kennel for long periods of time until they have been trained to stay in it. This will avoid them peeing in the kennel, which would be a bad habit to get started."

Jan Hill
Dark Knight Shibas

As mentioned, training starts from the moment your Shiba Inu becomes your responsibility. Considering the fact that your dog may be stubborn, you want to start getting your pup used to the idea that you are in charge. This will help play against the Shiba Inu's headstrong nature. Don't expect it to eliminate the behavior, but you can at least let your new pup know what the hierarchy is.

Puppies younger than six months old shouldn't be in the crate for hours at a time. They will not be able to hold their bladders that long, so

Photo Courtesy of
Caitlin Rubinstein

you need to make sure they have a way to get out and use the restroom in an acceptable place. If you get an adult dog that is not housetrained, you will need to follow the same rules.

Make sure that the door is set so that it doesn't close on your dog during his initial sniff of the crate. You don't want your Shiba Inu to get hit by the door as it is closing and scare him.

1. Let your Shiba Inu sniff the crate. Talk to him while he does this, using a positive, happy voice. Associate the first experience in the crate with excitement and positive emotions so that your dog understands it is a good place. If you have a blanket from the puppy's mother, put it in the crate to help provide an extra sense of comfort.

2. Drop a couple of treats into the crate if your canine seems reluctant to enter it. Do NOT force your dog into the crate. If your dog doesn't want to go all the way into this strange little space, that is perfectly fine. It has to be his decision to enter so that it isn't a negative experience.

3. Feed your dog in the crate for a week or two. This will help create some very positive emotions with the crate, as well as helping you to keep the food away from other pets if you have them.

   a. If your dog appears comfortable with the crate, put the food all the way at the back of the crate.

   b. If not, place the food bowl in the front, then move it further back in the crate over time.

4. Start closing the door once your dog appears to be eating comfortably in the crate. When the food is gone, open the crate immediately.

5. Leave the door closed for longer periods of time after your dog has eaten. If your pup begins to whine, you have left your Shiba Inu in the crate for too long.

6. Crate your dog for longer periods of time once your dog shows no signs of discomfort in the crate when he is eating. You can start to train him to go into the crate by simply saying "crate" or "bed," then praise your dog to let him know that he has done a great job.

Repeat this for several weeks until your dog feels comfortable in the crate. Doing this several times each day can help your dog to learn that everything is all right and that the crate is not a punishment. Initially, you will be doing this while you are still at home or when you go out to get the mail. As soon as your puppy can make it for half an hour without whining while you're out of the room, you can start leaving your pup alone while you are gone, keeping the time to no more than an hour in the beginning.

Once your dog understands not to tear up your home, the crate training is complete.

The focus during these first few weeks is to start housetraining and minimize any undesirable behavior. Training from the start is vital, but don't take your new puppy to any classes just yet. This is because most puppies have not had all of the necessary shots, and good trainers will not allow them in classes until the full first round of shots is complete. Chapters 10 and 12 provide a closer look at the different kinds of training you should begin and how to follow through after the first few weeks.

First Night Frights

That first night is going to be scary to your little Shiba Inu puppy. As understandable as this may be, there is only so much comfort you can give your new family member. Just like with a baby, the more you respond to cries and whimpering, the more you are teaching a puppy that negative behaviors will provide the desired results. You will need to be prepared for a balancing act to provide reassurance that things will be all right while keeping your puppy from learning that crying gets your attention.

Create a sleeping area just for your puppy near where you sleep. The area should have the puppy's bed tucked safely into a crate. It offers him a safe place to hide so that he can feel more comfortable in a strange new home. The entire area should be blocked off so that no one can get into it (and the puppy can't get out) during the night. It should also be close to where people sleep so that the puppy doesn't feel abandoned. If you were able to get a blanket or pillow that smells like the mother, make sure this is in your puppy's space. Consider adding a little white noise to cover unfamiliar sounds that could scare your new pet.

Your puppy will make noises over the course of the night. Don't move the puppy away, even if the whimpering keeps you awake. If you give in, over time the whimpering, whining, and crying will get louder. During the night, your puppy is not whimpering because he's been in the crate too long; he's scared or wants someone to be with him – he's probably never been alone at night before arriving at your home. Spare yourself some trouble later by teaching the puppy that whimpering doesn't always work to get him out of the crate. However, you should not move him either. Being moved away from people will only scare the puppy more, reinforcing the anxiety he feels. Over time, simply being close to you at night will be enough to reassure your puppy that everything will be all right.

Don't let your puppy into your bed until he is fully housetrained. Once a Shiba Inu learns that the bed is accessible, you can't train him not to hop up on it. And if he isn't housetrained, you'll need a new bed in the very near future.

Puppies will need to go to the bathroom every two to three hours, and you will need to get up during the night to make sure your puppy understands that he is to always go to the bathroom either outside or on the pee pad. If you let it go at night, you are going to have a difficult time training him that he cannot go in the house later.

Photo Courtesy of
Ann Nghiem

CHAPTER 8
The Multi-Pet Household

"Introduce your new puppy to other pets by having it in crate, and bring into area where other pets are, i.e. kitchen, living room. Be patient, do not let them all loose together until after enough time has elapsed for everyone to have their sniff, and calm down. If introducing to cats, be sure to give them a safe place to escape to. If introducing to elderly dogs, don't let the puppy be rude. A good role model elder will tell a puppy to calm down, don't discipline the older dog if it pins puppy, or warns it off."

Susan Norris-Jones
SunJo Shiba Inu & Japanese Chin

FURTHER READING
Ridiculous!

Nicholas, You Are Ridiculous! is an illustrated children's book that chronicles the adventures of a mischievous Shiba Inu. The book was published in 2009 by BookSurge Publishing and was illustrated by Olene Kassian. Kassian based the troublemaking pup on her own Shiba Inu named Nikki.

Shiba Inu do not tend to get along well with other alpha dogs – they really want to be in charge. However, if your dog or dogs are playful and don't have dominant tendencies, the introduction of a new Shiba Inu into your home tends to be fairly easy. They do enjoy playing rough, which may make them difficult to introduce to older dogs, so you will need to be careful.

Proper socialization is important for Shiba Inu. Having a dog already in your home can help your puppy become socialized earlier, as well as teach your puppy how things work in your home. Your new Shiba Inu may not choose to listen to you, but at least your pup will learn the rules. If your current dog or dogs have any undesirable behaviors, you may want to try to work those out before your puppy arrives, too – you don't want your Shiba Inu learning bad habits. Odds are he will come up with his own troubles to get into, but you don't need him getting ideas from other pets.

Introducing Your New Puppy To Your Other Pets

Always introduce all new dogs to your current dog or dogs, regardless of age, in a neutral place away from your home. Even if you have never had problems with your current dog, you are about to change his world. Select a park or other public area where your dog will not feel territorial and plan to introduce your dog to the puppy there. This gives the animals the opportunity to meet and get to know each other before entering your home together.

When introducing your dog and puppy, make sure you have at least one other adult with you so there's a person to manage each canine. If you have more than one dog, then you should have one adult per dog. This will make it easier to keep all of the dogs under control. Even the best dogs can get overly excited about meeting a puppy. One of the people who needs to be there is the person who is in charge of the pets in your home (or people if you have more than one person in charge). This helps establish the pack hierarchy.

Don't hold your puppy when the dogs meet. While you may want to protect the puppy and make him feel comfortable by holding him, it has the opposite effect. Your puppy will likely feel trapped, with no way to escape. Being on the ground means that the puppy can run if he feels the need to. Stand near the puppy with your feet a little bit apart. That way, if the puppy decides he needs to escape he can quickly hide behind your legs.

*Photo Courtesy of
Trisha Cutright*

Photo Courtesy of Sheryl Royalty

Watch for raised hackles on your dog. The puppy and each dog should have a few minutes to sniff each other, making sure that there is always some slack in the leash. This helps them feel more relaxed since they won't feel like you are trying to restrain them. Your dog will probably either want to play or will simply ignore the puppy.

- If they want to play, just be careful that the dog doesn't accidentally hurt the puppy.
- If the dog ends up ignoring the puppy after an initial sniff, that is fine too.

If your dog's hackles are up or if he is clearly unhappy, keep them apart until your dog seems more comfortable with the situation. Don't force the meeting.

The introduction could take a while, depending on individual dog personalities. The friendlier and more accepting your dog is, the easier it will be to incorporate your new puppy into the home. For some dogs a week is enough time to start feeling comfortable together. For other dogs, it could take a couple of months before they are fully accepting of a new puppy. Since this is a completely new dynamic in your household, your current dog may not be pleased with you bringing a little bundle of energy into his daily life. This is enough to make anyone unhappy, but especially a dog that has grown accustomed to a certain lifestyle. The older your dog is, the more likely it is that a puppy will be an unwelcome addition. Older dogs can get cranky around a puppy that doesn't understand the rules or doesn't seem to know when enough is enough. The goal is to make your puppy feel welcome and safe, while letting your older dog know that your love for him is just as strong as ever.

Once your new family member and the rest of the canine pack start to get acquainted and feel comfortable with each other, you can head home. As they enter the house, they will have a bit more familiarity with each other, making your current dogs feel more comfortable with the new addition to the family.

Once you are home, take the dogs into the yard and remove the leashes. You will need one adult per dog, including the puppy. If they seem to be all right or the dog is indifferent to the puppy, you can let your dog inside, re-leash the puppy, and keep the puppy on the leash as you go inside.

Put the puppy in the puppy area when the introductions are done.

Introducing An Adult Dog To Other Animals

You always need to approach the introduction and first few weeks with caution. The new adult Shiba Inu will need his own stuff in the beginning, and should be kept in a separate area when you aren't around until you know that there won't be any fighting. If your dogs don't have much interest in being the boss and enjoy playing rough, it will take less time for your new Shiba Inu to fit into the pack.

Plan for the introduction to take at least an hour. It probably won't take that long, but you must make sure that all of the dogs are comfort-

Photo Courtesy of
Brooke Steinbach

able during the introduction. Since the dogs are all adults, they will need to move at their own pace.

Follow the same steps to introduce your current dogs with your new dog as you would with a puppy.

- Start on neutral territory.
- Have one adult human per dog present at the introduction (this is even more important when introducing an adult canine).
- Introduce one dog at a time – don't let several dogs meet your new Shiba Inu at the same time. Having multiple dogs approaching all at once in an unfamiliar environment with people the Shiba Inu doesn't know very well – you can probably see how this can be nerve-racking for any new dog.

Unlike with a puppy, make sure to bring treats to the meeting of two adults dogs. The animals will respond well to the treats, and you will have a way to quickly distract all of the dogs if they are too tense with each other.

During the introduction, watch the Shiba Inu and your dogs to see if any of them raises his hackles. This is one of the first really obvious signs that a dog is uncomfortable. If the Shiba Inu's hackles are up, back off the introductions for a little bit. Do this by calling your current dog back first. This is also when you should start waving treats around. Avoid pulling on the leashes to separate the dogs. You don't want to add physical tension to the situation because that could trigger a fight. Treats will work for all dogs present in the beginning, and your other dogs should be able to respond to your calling their names.

If any of the dogs are showing their teeth or growling, call your dog back and give the dogs a chance to settle down first. Use the treats and a calming voice to get them to relax. You want all the dogs to feel comfortable during the first meeting, so you can't force the friendship. If they seem uncomfortable or wary at first, you will need to let them move at their own pace.

Older Dogs And Your Shiba Inu

If your current dog is older, keep in mind that puppies are energetic and likely to keep trying to engage the older dog in play. This can be very trying for your older canine. Make sure that your older dog isn't getting too tired of the puppy's antics because you don't want your puppy to learn to snap at other dogs. Watch for signs that your older dog is ready for some alone time, some time alone with you, or just a break from the puppy.

Once your Shiba Inu is ready to leave the puppy area for good, you will still want to make sure that your older dog has safe places to go to be

Photo Courtesy of
Whitney Kono

alone in case he just doesn't feel up to being around a spry young thing. This will reduce the likelihood that your puppy will be repeatedly scolded and therefore learn to be wary of older dogs.

Even if you adopt an adult Shiba Inu, they tend to like to play rough with other dogs. This can be a problem with older dogs, so make sure that your dog's golden years aren't marred by a new canines that has rules that don't make sense to your older dog and wants to play in a way your older dog can't.

Dog Aggression And Territorial Behaviors

"Lack of exercise is #1 reason for issues such as barking, chewing, scratching, aggression."

Susan Norris-Jones
SunJo Shiba Inu & Japanese Chin

When out of the home, Shiba Inu are really not a problem. Some people have classified the breed as aggressive because they will snap at dogs who get too enthusiastic or in-your-face. This is a breed that likes to be in charge and is quite independent. Just as you would not react well to someone crowding your personal space and being too friendly, a Shiba

Inu may snap when another dog invades his space. This is not a true act of aggression, more of a warning that the dog is acting in a way that the Shiba Inu doesn't like. Once the dog backs off, your Shiba Inu will probably entirely lose interest. This is very different than a dog that is aggressive because an aggressive dog will continue to try to get to the other dog. A Shiba Inu just wants to have his own personal space. Once that is achieved, he probably will go back to acting normal. It is your job to make sure other people know to keep their overeager dogs from getting too up close and personal with your dog.

Do not use choke chains or other negative reinforcers on your Shiba Inu. Not only do those hurt your dog, they don't work well. A Shiba Inu does not react well to negative reinforcement because he thinks for himself. What you teach your Shiba Inu with these types of restraints is that you don't know what you are doing and are using things to try to force your dog to behave in a certain way. What does work are treats and removal from any negative situation. Reward your dog for the good behavior, and the more often your dog does what you want him to do, the more often you reward him. Chapter 12 goes into how to train your Shiba Inu.

At home, you will need to be more careful. Because this is a dog that likes to be in charge, you need to watch for aggressive behavior. Despite his size, a Shiba Inu is not the kind of dog to back down, so if he feels that someone is challenging him or taking one of his toys, he may react aggressively. While he is young, it is easier to start to train against this kind of be-

Photo Courtesy of Rachel Deihl

havior, but an older dog will need extra monitoring and should not be left alone with other pets or children. An older Shiba Inu has to learn how to be a part of the pack and the proper way to react to people playing with toys and other items. This is why it is essential to always be firm and consistent.

There are two primary types of aggression that you should monitor for in your dog.

- Dominance aggression is when your dog wants to demonstrate control over another animal or person. This kind of aggression is shown through the following behaviors in reaction to anyone going near the Shiba Inu's belongings (like toys or a food bowl):
  - Growling
  - Nipping
  - Snapping

  This is the behavior that the pack leader makes to warn others in the pack about touching his stuff. If your Shiba Inu reacts like this toward you, a family member, or another pet going close to his stuff, you must intervene immediately, correct him by saying "No," then lavish him with praise when he stops. You must consistently intervene whenever your Shiba Inu behaves in this manner.

  Do not let the Shiba Inu be alone with other people, dogs, or animals as long as any of this type of behavior is exhibited. He will push boundaries, and if you aren't there to intervene, he will likely try to show his dominance in your absence. You want to train your Shiba Inu not to react aggressively. Once you are sure the behavior has been eliminated, you can leave your dog and Shiba Inu alone for short periods of time, with you staying in another room or somewhere in close proximity, but out of sight. Over time, you can start to leave your pets alone when you go get the mail, then when you run errands. Eventually, you will be able to leave your Shiba Inu alone with other dogs without worrying that he or one of your other dogs will feel compelled to show dominance.

- Well socialized males are more interested in meeting and greeting other dogs. Unsocialized males can be aggressive and domineering. Females tend to be more predictable; they are more aloof even when properly socialized, but they are less likely to be as aggressive or domineering when not socialized.

Your Shiba Inu will have to learn that the home is not just his. It belongs to people and the other dogs as well, and he is a part of the home, not the boss in your home.

Strong Natural Prey Drive

Over much of the history of the breed, Shiba Inu have chased other animals. After centuries of chasing prey, they naturally have a high prey drive. You will need to plan to socialize your Shiba Inu puppy with the cat long before the puppy is allowed to run free in the home. Always be present when they interact so that you can correct the puppy's behavior. If you bring an adult Shiba Inu into the home, monitor the interaction. Since cats are about the same size as some Shiba Inu, there isn't a great risk of the Shiba Inu trying to chase the cat, but he may react like he would to another dog.

If you have other small animals, they will need to be kept in areas where your Shiba Inu cannot go. Rabbits, ferrets, and other pets typically are not trainable. Most small animals aren't able to learn not to run away, which your puppy will likely take as an invitation to play. Since smaller animals are usually in containers, this will make them less interesting to your Shiba Inu. It is more when you are outside that you have to be more careful of your Shiba Inu's natural drive to chase. This means that you really should not allow your Shiba Inu off-leash without fencing. Even if you do have fencing, you will need to keep a close eye on your dog. If a small animal catches your Shiba Inu's eyes, his attention will be focused on catching the animal, and fences are not as much of a deterrent as you might think they are. This is a breed that can problem solve, so escaping from a fenced-in area is not that much of a challenge.

Feeding Time Practices

Your Shiba Inu puppy will be fed in the puppy space, so mealtime will not be a problem in the beginning. When you start to feed the puppy with the other dogs, you can use the following instructions to reduce the chance of territorial behavior with food.

1. Feed your Shiba Inu at the same time as the other dogs, but in a different room than your other dogs. Keeping them separated will let your Shiba Inu eat without distraction or feeling that your other dogs will eat what is in his bowl. Make sure to feed your Shiba Inu in the same room each time, while the other dogs eat in their established room or rooms.

2. Keep your Shiba Inu and other dogs to their areas until they finish eating their food. Some dogs have a tendency to leave food in the bowl. Don't let them. They need to finish everything in the bowl be-

cause all food bowls will be removed as soon as the dogs are done eating to remove the need to protect those bowls.

3. Make sure you have someone near your Shiba Inu so that he learns not to growl at people near the bowl. This will help to reduce stress when other dogs are around the food. If your dog demonstrates any aggression, immediately correct him by saying "No," then give him praise when he stops. Do not attempt to play with the food bowl, and make sure none of the kids play with it. Your dog needs to know that no one is going to try to steal his food.

4. Move the dogs closer together over a couple of weeks. For example, you can feed your current dog on one side of the door near the doorway and the Shiba Inu on the opposite side near the doorway.

5. After a month or two, you can feed them in the same room, but with some distance between them. If the Shiba Inu starts to exhibit protective behavior with the other dogs, correct him, then praise him when he stops the behavior.

Eventually, you can start feeding the dogs close together. It can take weeks to months, depending on the age of the Shiba Inu when he comes to your home. A puppy will require less time because he will be socialized with the dogs from an early age, making him less wary. That does not mean that he won't display territorial behavior, but it likely won't take long for him to start to feel comfortable eating near the rest of the pack.

For adults, it could take longer, and you should not rush it. Let your dog learn to feel comfortable eating before you make changes, even small ones. Dogs of any breed can be protective of their food, depending on what they have been through; this is exacerbated in protective breeds like the Shiba Inu. Your Shiba Inu needs to feel assured that this protective behavior is not necessary around other dogs before he will eat without incident. That means letting his confidence and comfort build at his own pace.

A Little Extra Cleaning

Shiba Inu are one of the cleanest breeds of canines, and will groom themselves about as often as a cat. Some Shiba Inu will take this a step further and will start to clean other dogs, and sometimes cats. It isn't something that is likely to be a problem, especially if your other dogs like the attention. At the end of the day, it could be a nice way for them to bond. It also can help to keep some of your other dogs a bit cleaner. Of course, this will not replace bathing and brushing, but it is nice to see a dog interested in helping to keep things a little cleaner.

CHAPTER 9
The First Few Weeks

"Don't be offended if they don't want to be cuddled. Most Shibas don't like to be restrained."

Vicki DeBerry
DeBerry Shiba Inu

Your Shiba Inu puppy is probably going to spend most of his first week at his new home moving between being excited and being nervous (although the majority of his time will be spent sleeping). After learning that your home is his home, your pup will start to exhibit more personality and interest in his new world. While his intellect will probably make your puppy easy to housetrain, it will also mean you are more likely to have a bored puppy that gets into trouble. One of the most important things you will do during this time is ensure that your puppy feels safe and comfortable. He will need a lot of attention and care to let him know that he is where he belongs.

The bond you start to build in that first week will continue to develop over the first month. By the end of the month, your pup should be sleeping through the night and may have a fairly good understanding of where to go to the bathroom. You will also have a pretty good understanding of your canine's personality, which will make it a lot easier to know how to comfort the puppy during his infrequent bouts of uncertainty.

The first month is when you really need to start paying attention to your puppy's emerging personality. With a Shiba Inu, this will probably be when you start to notice his independent streak. If this happens, you have to start learning with your puppy. It cannot be a power struggle, and you definitely should not start using any kind of negative reinforcement to assert your dominance. If your Shiba Inu starts to act more independent, you will need to learn how to react without turning it into a big deal. As much as possible, this is the time to begin gradually working to stop or reduce any undesirable behaviors.

The key during this time is to remain consistent. Use what you learn about your puppy's personality to encourage good behavior.

Setting The Rules And Sticking To Them

Your puppy needs to understand the rules and know that you and your family mean them. A firm, consistent approach is best for both you and your dog. If you don't remain consistent, you are setting yourself and your Shiba Inu up for a lot of contention that will make everyone miserable. Once your canine learns to listen to you, training your Shiba Inu to do tricks will still be up to your dog's mood, but he will be more excited if he learns early that you are in charge.

Photo Courtesy of Kristi Wiegraffe

Photo Courtesy of
Pervie Villareal

Establish A No Jumping And No Mouthing Policy

"Biting - this is normal play behavior for a Shiba puppy, but it needs to be discouraged with humans, and especially children. Mouthing is acceptable, but teeth should not be felt."

Susan Norris-Jones
SunJo Shiba Inu & Japanese Chin

You will need to train your newest family member not to do certain puppy things, like nipping and jumping. Even if they aren't known for being aggressive and a Shiba Inu isn't likely to be able to knock you down, you still don't want him to learn bad habits.

Nipping
- One of the triggers for nipping is overstimulation, which can be one of the signs that your puppy is too tired to keep playing or training and you should put him to bed.

- Another trigger could be that your canine has too much energy. If this is the case, take your puppy outside to burn off some of his excess energy. At the same time, be careful not to over-exercise the puppy.

You need to be vigilant and immediately let your puppy know that nipping is not acceptable. Some people recommend using a water spritzer bottle and spraying the puppy while saying "No" after nipping. This is one of the few times when punishment may be effective, but you need to be careful not to associate it with anything other than the nipping.

Always tell your puppy "No" firmly whenever he is nipping, even if it is during playtime. You should also pull away and say "Ouch!" loudly to let your puppy know that his teeth are hurting you. This will help to establish the idea that nipping is bad and is never rewarded.

Chewing
All puppies chew to relieve the pain of teething. Chewing can be an expensive problem for your dog to have, but it is fairly common with this breed. Whether he is chewing your furniture, utensils, or clothing, you want to discourage this behavior as quickly as possible.
- Make sure you have toys for your Shiba Inu (either adult or puppy) so that you can teach him what things are acceptable to chew on.

*Photo Courtesy of
Janice Hill
Darknight Shibas*

Having a lot of available toys, and rotating those toys out, will help give your puppy or dog a variety of options.

- If your puppy is teething, either refrigerate a couple of toys so they are cold, or give your puppy frozen carrots. The cold will help numb the pain.

- Toys that are made either of hard rubber or hard nylon will be the best toys, particularly Kongs with kibble in them. You can even fill them with water and freeze them, which will give your puppy something cool to sooth the pain.

For the most part, keeping your eye on your dog when he is not in his designated space will help you to quickly see when he is chewing on things he shouldn't. When this happens, say "No" firmly. If your dog continues to chew, put him back in his space. While he is in the space, make sure he has plenty of toys to chew on.

If you decide to use chew deterrents, be aware that some dogs will not care that an item tastes bad – they will chew anyway. Do not apply these deterrents and then leave your dog alone and expect him to just stop chewing. You need to see your dog's reaction before trusting that the bad habit is broken.

Jumping

Dogs typically jump on people when they first greet them. Use the following steps when you have a visitor (and if you can get someone who is willing to help, that will make the training that much easier).

1. Put a leash on the dog when the person knocks on the door or rings the bell. The arrival of someone else will invariably excite most dogs, especially puppies.

2. Let the person in, but do not approach the person with the puppy until he calms down.

3. Be effusive in your praise when the puppy keeps all four paws on the ground. Approach the visitor only after your Shiba Inu is calm.

4. When the puppy jumps up, turn your body and ignore him. Don't verbally correct him. Being completely ignored will be far more of a deterrent than any words you can say.

5. Give your dog something to hold in his mouth if he does not settle down. Sometimes dogs just need a task to reduce their excitement. A stuffed animal or ball are ideal for distraction, even if your dog drops it.

6. Get low and pet your dog. Having someone on his level will make him feel like he is being included. It also lets him sniff your face, which is part of a proper greeting. If your visitor is willing to help, this obvious acknowledgment can be a deterrent from jumping as the person is already on your dog's level.

Reward-Based Training Vs Discipline-Based Training

Other chapters detail the various aspects of training, but it is important to keep in mind just how much more efficient it is to train with rewards than with punishments, especially for an intelligent breed like the Shiba Inu. This will be a particular challenge as puppies can be exuberant and are easily distracted. It is important to remember that your puppy is young, so you need to keep your temper and learn when you need to take a break from training.

Several critical aspects that you will need to start working on during the first month:

- Housetraining (Chapter 10)
- Crate training (Chapter 7)
- Barking (Chapter 12)
- Protection (you won't start this during the first month, but you will need to start gauging for it if you want your dog to be an ideal protector) (Chapter 12)

Find out how much the breeder did in terms of housetraining and other such areas. The best breeders may even teach puppies one or two commands before they go home with you. If this is the case, keep using those same commands with your puppy so that the early training is not lost. This can help you establish the right tone of voice to use since the puppy will already know what the words mean and how to react to them. Once he understands that, he will more quickly pick up on other uses of that tone of voice as being the way you talk when you are training. It is another great way to let your little love know when you mean business versus when you want to play. These kinds of distinctions are easily picked up by Shiba Inu and your dog will be more than happy to oblige.

Separation Anxiety In Dogs And Puppies

Some Shiba Inu suffer from separation anxiety, and many of them don't much care for changes in the schedule. Even those that don't feel so upset about being left alone may tear up your home out of boredom. As a breed with a history of working, if you give your Shiba Inu something to do while you are gone, the feeling of separation won't be quite so intense; he will mostly just get bored. Still, it is a problem that you are likely to encounter, so you need to plan ahead to help your puppy understand that your being gone doesn't mean you won't return.

In the beginning, keep the puppy's time alone to a minimum. The sounds of people moving around the house will help your Shiba Inu understand that the separation is not permanent. After the first week or so, alone time can involve you going out to get the mail, leaving the puppy inside by himself for just a few minutes. You can then lengthen the amount of time you are away from the puppy over a few days until the puppy is alone for 30 minutes or so at a time.

Here are some basic guidelines for when you first start to leave your puppy alone.

- Take the puppy out about 30 minutes before you leave.
- Tire the puppy out with exercise or playtime so that your leaving is not such a big deal.
- Place the puppy in the puppy area well ahead of when you go out to avoid having him associate the space with something bad happening.
- Don't give your puppy extra attention right before you leave because that reinforces the idea that you give attention before something bad happens.
- Avoid reprimanding your Shiba Inu for any behavior that happens while you are away. Reprimanding teaches him to be more stressed because it will seem like you come home angry.

If your Shiba Inu exhibits signs of separation anxiety, there are several things you can do to help make him comfortable during your absence.

- Chew toys can give your dog something acceptable to gnaw on while you are away.
- A blanket or shirt that smells like you or other family members can help provide comfort too. If you have worn the item and haven't gotten it very dirty, this is ideal, just make sure that you were not in contact with any chemicals over the course of the day you wore it. You also need to make sure that your dog won't eat the item in your ab-

93

Photo Courtesy of
Ann Nghiem

sence. Consider giving him something that you know you won't wear again, in case he shreds it to pieces.

- Leave the area well lit, even if it is during the day. Should something happen and you get home later than you intended to, you don't want your little guy to be in the dark.

- Turn on a stereo (classical music is best) or television (old-timey shows that don't have loud noises, like Mr. Ed or I Love Lucy) so that the house isn't completely quiet and unfamiliar noises are less obvious.

FUN FACT
News Anchor Shiba

Inuyama Shibao plays a Japanese news anchor for SBK News in a series of infomercials for 7-11 Banking Services in Japan. He is also a Shiba Inu! Inuyama has gained internet celebrity status for his dashing suits and playful mannerisms while he pretends to read the news.

It will not take your Shiba Inu long to notice the kind of behaviors that indicate you are leaving. Grabbing your keys, purse, wallet, and other indications will quickly become triggers that can make your Shiba Inu anxious because he is going to quickly learn what these actions mean. Don't make a big deal out of it. If you act in a normal way, over time this will help your little one to understand that your leaving is fine and that everything will be all right.

How Long Is Too Long To Be Left Home Alone?

Though they are very independent dogs, Shiba Inu don't do well when left home alone for long periods of time. About eight hours is all they can manage before they start to get anxious, bored, or annoyed. This may require that you leave your pup this long in a crate in the early days, but over time your goal should be to allow your dog to be out of the crate so that it doesn't feel like a punishment. Your companion will not do well being trapped in a crate for hours at a time. You need to find some good mental games or things that your pup can do while you are gone to keep your Shiba Inu from being destructive. This is also why it is vital to ensure that you have your home properly prepared prior to your dog's arrival, especially if you get an adult Shiba Inu. Once your dog is crate trained and you start trying to leave him alone for longer periods of time, you want to make sure any destructive urges are put in check as much as possible.

Don't Overdo It, Physically Or Mentally

A tired puppy is a lot like a tired toddler; you have to keep the little guy from becoming exhausted or overworking those little legs. You need to be careful about harming your puppy's growing bones. Your pup is probably going to think that sleep is unnecessary, no matter how tired he is. It is up to you to read the signs that tell you when to stop all activities and put your pup to bed or take a break.

Training needs to be conducted in increments of time that your puppy or dog can handle. Be careful that you aren't pushing the training past the puppy's concentration threshold or that you aren't discouraging your adult dog with commands that are too advanced for him. If you continue training past your puppy's energy levels, the lessons learned are not going to be the ones you want to teach your dog. At this age, training sessions don't need to be long, they just need to be consistent.

Walks will be much shorter during that first month. When you go out, stay within a few blocks of home. Don't worry – by the month's end, your puppy will have a lot more stamina so you can enjoy longer walks and short trips away from home if needed. By the end of the first year you

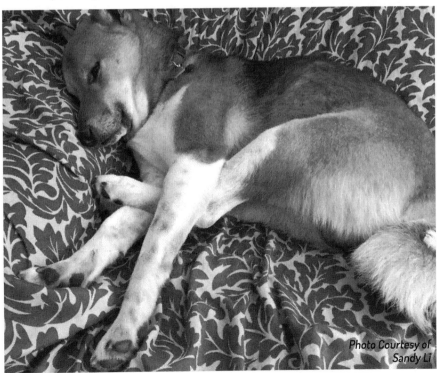

Photo Courtesy of
Sandy Li

96

should be able to go for a short jog, depending on the advice from your vet. You can also do a bit of running on the leash in the yard if your puppy has a lot of extra energy. This will help your Shiba Inu learn how to behave on the leash while running. Puppies have a tendency to want to attack the leash because it is a distraction from running freely.

Just because your puppy can't take long walks initially doesn't mean that he won't have plenty of energy. Daily exercise will be essential, with the caveat that you need to make sure your puppy isn't doing too much, too soon. Staying active will help him to not only be healthy, but keep him mentally stimulated. You will quickly realize just how sedentary you have been if you have never had a dog before because you will be on the move almost all of the time the puppy is awake.

CHAPTER 10
Housetraining

"Shibas potty train easily, as long as owners are consistent, and persistent! Crate them when you are not specifically paying attention to them and take them outside as soon as they wake up from a nap, and after meals."

CJ Strehle
JADE Shiba Inu

Housetraining a puppy isn't really any more difficult or time consuming than potty training a toddler, and with a Shiba Inu, it is actually a bit easier. It is important to set a schedule and then not deviate from it. Your new family member will want a clean area and will quickly learn to let you know when he needs to go.

Using a leash can be very helpful in ensuring that your puppy learns when and where to go, but there will still be challenges as you work to establish the hierarchy and convince your puppy to listen to you.

Make sure to consistently apply these two rules.

1.   Never let the puppy roam the home alone – they should always be in the dedicated puppy space when you aren't watching them. Dogs don't like having a dirty bed, so your pup is much less likely to have accidents in his crate or near his bedding in the dedicated space. Your Shiba Inu won't be pleased with the idea of being in a soiled crate, so that is a deterrent from using the bathroom when you are not around. He may not take the same approach to other areas of the home if he is left free to wander.

RESOURCE
Shiba Inu Rescue Association (SIRA)

The Shiba Inu Rescue Association (SIRA) is a 501(c)3 based in the Midwest. SIRA is a volunteer-run organization that rescues Shiba Inu and Shiba mixes from situations where they are neglected, abandoned, or abused. After a screening process, the dogs are placed in foster homes where the dogs are rehabilitated and prepared for life in their new forever homes. For more information about this organization, visit their website at www.savingshibas.com.

2. Give your puppy constant, easy access to the locations where you plan to housetrain him. You will need to make frequent trips outside as your puppy learns where to do his business, particularly if constant access to a place to use the restroom isn't possible. When you go out, put a leash on your puppy to make sure you make a point of where in the yard you want him to use the bathroom.

Always begin with a training plan, then be even stricter with yourself than you are with your puppy to keep that schedule. You are the key to the puppy learning where it is acceptable to do his business.

Inside Or Outside – Housetraining Options And Considerations

If your breeder has already started housetraining the puppy, stick to the method that was used.

You have the following housetraining options for your puppy:

- Pee pads – You should have several around the home for training, including in the puppy's area, but as far from the bed as possible.
- Regular outings outside – Organize these based on your puppy's sleeping and eating schedule.

Photo Courtesy of
Gabe & Natty Hynes

- Rewards – You can use treats in the beginning, but quickly shift to praise.

In the beginning, the best way to housetrain your dog is by going out a lot of times, including at night, so that your puppy learns to keep all of his business outside. During the first few months, it is best to use a leash when you take the puppy out. This will help him learn to walk on a leash and keep him from getting distracted before he does his business.

A word of warning – don't start praising the puppy until the puppy is done going to the bathroom. Interrupting mid-potty may make the puppy stop, increasing the odds that he will go again after you get back inside.

Setting A Schedule

You need to keep an eye on your puppy and consistently have house-training sessions:

- After eating
- After waking up from sleeping or each nap
- On a schedule (after it has been established)

Watch your Shiba Inu for cues like sniffing and circling, two very common activities as a puppy searches for a place to go. Start tailoring your schedule around your puppy's unique needs.

Puppies have small bladders and little control in the early days. If you have to train your pup to go inside, there needs to be a single designated space with a clean pee pad in the puppy area, and you need to stock up on the appropriate pads for the puppy to have somewhere to go that isn't the floor. Then make sure you change those pads regularly so your puppy does not get accustomed to having waste nearby. The pads are better than newspaper and can absorb more. You will need to plan to transition to having him do his business outdoors as quickly as possible, but that should not be too much of a problem with a Shiba Inu.

Choosing A Location

"Plan how to get puppy outside to go potty - this is a clean breed that is often house trained by 7 weeks, and will NOT go potty indoors. And be prepared to take puppy outside every 4 hours during the day - rain or shine."

Susan Norris-Jones
SunJo Shiba Inu & Japanese Chin

Photo Courtesy of
Ann Nghiem

A designated restroom space can help make the experience of house training easier because the Shiba Inu will begin to associate one area of the yard for that one purpose, rather than sniffing around until he finds a choice spot. Having him go in one spot regularly will also make cleanup much simpler too; that way you can continue to use the whole yard instead of having to worry about stepping in waste whenever you or anyone else goes outside.

When you are out for walks is the perfect time to train your puppy to go to the bathroom. Between walks and the yard, your puppy will come to see the leash as a sign that it is time to relieve his bladder, which could become a Pavlovian response. Given that Shiba Inu are so smart, it won't take your companion long to understand the correlation.

Make sure that you pay attention to your puppy the entire time you are outside. You need to make sure that he understands the purpose of going outside is to go to the bathroom. Do not send your puppy outside and assume that he's done what you wanted him to do. Until there are no more accidents in the home, you need to verify that your puppy isn't losing focus while he is outside.

Keyword Training

All training should include keywords, even housetraining. You and all members of the family should know what words to use when training your dog where to go to the bathroom, and you should all be using those words consistently. If you have paired an adult with a child, the adult should be the one using the keyword during training.

To avoid confusing your puppy, be careful not to select words that you often use inside the home. Use a phrase like "Get busy" to let your puppy know it's time to get to work, not something that involves the word bathroom or potty – these are words that you will probably say inside, which could trigger him to go when you don't mean for him to go. "Get busy" is not a phrase most people use in their daily routine, so it is not something you are likely to say when you don't mean for your puppy to use the bathroom.

Once your puppy learns to use the bathroom based on the command, make sure he finishes before offering praise or rewards.

Reward Good Behavior With Positive Reinforcement

Positive reinforcement is unbelievably effective with Shiba Inu. In the beginning, take a few pieces of kibble with you when you are teaching your puppy where to go, both inside and outside the home. Learning that you are the one in charge will help teach the Shiba Inu to look to you for cues and instructions.

Part of being consistent with training means lavishing the little guy with praise whenever your puppy does the right thing. If you gently lead your puppy to the area on a leash without any other stops, it will gradually become obvious that your Shiba Inu should go there to use the bathroom. Once you get outside, encourage your Shiba Inu to go when you get to the place in the yard that is intended to be his bathroom spot. As soon as he does his business, give him immediate and very enthusiastic praise. Pet your puppy as you talk to let the little guy know just how good the action was. Once the praise is done, return inside immediately. This is not playtime. You want your puppy to associate certain outings with designated potty time.

Praise is far more effective for Shiba Inu, but you can also give your puppy a treat after a few successful trips outside. Definitely do not make treats a habit after each trip because you do not want your Shiba Inu to expect one every time he does his business. The lesson is to go outside, and that may include treats. Most Shiba Inu will be satisfied with simply keeping their area clean, so your little guy will not need treats for long once he becomes accustomed to going outside.

The best way to train in the first month or two is to go out every hour or two, even at night. You will need to set an alarm to wake you within that time to take the puppy outside. Use the leash to keep the focus on using the bathroom, give the same enthusiastic praise, then immediately return inside and go to bed. It is difficult, but your Shiba Inu will get the hang of it a lot faster if there isn't a long period between potty breaks. Over time, the pup will need to go out less frequently, giving you more rest.

If your Shiba Inu has an accident, it is important to refrain from punishing the puppy. Accidents are not a reason to punish – it really reflects more on your training and schedule than on what the puppy has learned. That said, accidents are pretty much an inevitability. When it happens, tell your puppy, "No. Potty outside!" and clean up the mess immediately. Once that is done take the puppy outside to go potty. Of course, if your puppy doesn't go, he doesn't get any praise.

Cleaning Up

Clean up any messes in the home as soon as you find them. Unless you see your puppy using the bathroom in the home, there is no point in negative reinforcement. Your dog will simply learn to hide his mess to avoid being punished. Take the dog outside instead and see if he will use the bathroom. If someone is home, it is best to clean up the mess as quickly as possible. Spend a bit of time researching what kinds of cleaner you want to use, whether generic or holistic. Shiba Inu don't have an issue with marking their territory, especially if they are properly trained, but you may want to discourage visiting dogs from claiming areas where your puppy had accidents. Enzyme cleaners are the best for cleaning up puppy accidents.

Pay attention to when these accidents happen and determine if there is a commonality between them. Perhaps you need to add an additional trip outside for your puppy or should make a change in his walking schedule. Or maybe there is something that is startling your dog, causing an accident.

CHAPTER 11
Socialization

The Shiba Inu is a dignified breed that doesn't exhibit any hint of fear. When not properly socialized, they can suffer from anxiety and fear, which will make them more aggressive towards other dogs. Since they are escape artists, you absolutely need to make sure that you socialize your puppy so that in the event of an escape your Shiba Inu isn't at greater risks. Also, a poorly socialized Shiba Inu is more likely to escape, even if that seems counter intuitive. Because he is a member of your family, you want your Shiba Inu to be happy around other people and dogs and to learn that the vast majority of them are not a threat, even if they don't recognize that your Shiba Inu is the boss.

Socialization allows your Shiba Inu puppy to learn that it can be a lot of fun to play with people you invite into your home and dogs that you encounter out on your walks – if your Shiba Inu is in the mood for inter-action. To make sure your Shiba Inu is comfortable, you have to plan to start socialization from a very early age.

Remember that your puppy will need to have all of his vaccinations before being exposed to other dogs.

Photo Courtesy of
Whitney Kono

Photo Courtesy of
Diane Leighton

Socialization Can Make Life Easier In The Long Run

All dogs need socialization, but intelligent breeds have more analytical minds, so you want them to learn as early as possible that most of the time the world is safe and that other people and animals usually don't pose a threat. It will also help you for your puppy to learn that acting in a dominant, aggressive way is not acceptable.

The benefit of early socialization is that it can make life that much more enjoyable for everyone involved, no matter what the situation is. A socialized dog will approach the world from a much better place than a dog that is not socialized.

Most Shiba Inu that aren't properly socialized will want to dominate other dogs. They aren't seeking to fight the dogs they encounter, but they want the other dogs to know that they are the boss. This will make going outside less enjoyable, and could be harmful to your Shiba Inu if he manages to escape your home.

Greeting New People

FUN FACT
Kabosu the Doge

Perhaps one of the first Shiba Inu to take the internet by storm was Kabosu. This adorable Shiba Inu is often credited as starting the Shiba Inu "doge" meme trend in 2013. Kabosu was rescued from a puppy mill in 2008 by Atsuko Sato, a kindergarten teacher, who posted pictures of her puppy online in order to spread awareness of the dangers of the puppy mill industry. Atsuko Sato did not start the meme trend, however. Instead, a third party found the pictures of Kabosu online and began posting them with the now-famous "doge" captions.

Training your Shiba Inu how to treat visitors may take a little longer because he may not be in the mood for any social interaction – and people are going to want to pet your adorable little dog. It will be just as important to let people know how to interact with your dog as it is to train your dog how to interact with visitors. Let your visitors know to leave the dog alone if the dog is not showing any interest in an introduction.

Puppies will likely enjoy meeting new people, so make sure to invite people over to help socialize your canine family member. To introduce your puppy to a new person, try one of these methods:

1. Try to have your puppy meet new people daily, if possible. This could be during walks or while you are doing other activities where you get out of the house. If you can't meet new people daily, try for at least 4 times a week.

2. Invite friends and family over, and let them spend a few minutes just giving the puppy attention. If your puppy has a favorite game or activity, let people know so that they can play with him. This will win the little guy over very quickly and teach him that new people are fun and safe.

3. Once your puppy is old enough to learn tricks (after the first month – don't try to teach him tricks immediately), have your little friend demonstrate the tricks for visitors. This will be really important as your puppy gets bigger because a lot of people are nervous around dogs of any size. A display of tricks helps them see that your dog is just as clownish and playful as other dogs.

4. Avoid crowds for the first few months. When your puppy is several months to a year old, attend some dog-friendly events so that your pup can learn not to be uncomfortable around a large group of people.

Photo Courtesy of
Trisha Cutright

Greeting New Dogs

"Shibas can be (and often are) dog aggressive, even with proper training."

CJ Strehle
JADE Shiba Inu

Chapter 8 covers the introduction of your new Shiba Inu with your other dogs, but meeting other dogs is a little different. Most dogs will bow and sniff each other during an introduction. Watch for the same signs of aggression covered in Chapter 8, such as raised hackles and bared teeth. Bowing, high tail, and perked ears usually mean that your Shiba Inu is excited about meeting the dog. If your Shiba Inu is making noises, watch for the signs of aggression to make sure that the sounds are of play, not unease.

One thing that most Shiba Inu do not like is another dog invading their space without warning. A dog coming up behind them and sniffing could trigger an aggressive response, if you Shiba Inu did not realize the dog was coming up. This will likely be more of a problem as your dog ages and does not hear or see so well. While young, you can warn people with overexcited dogs not to let their dog get too close to yours.

Be careful and slow about the introduction. It is possible your Shiba Inu won't want to be sniffed from behind, in which case make sure to block other dogs from going behind your dog.

The Importance Of Continuing Socialization

Socialization is never done with any dog, especially a dog as independent as a Shiba Inu. Making sure the puppy gets exposure to other people and other dogs is going to be important to keep him from getting too aggressive or dominant. This doesn't mean forcing him into interaction, but joining classes and setting up play dates will give your dog a reason to be excited about meeting others.

You don't have to leave home though if you don't want to. Have family and friends visit regularly, especially bringing their dogs along, so that your Shiba Inu has constant reminders that his home is a welcoming place, not somewhere that he needs to exert his dominance. You don't want your pup to feel that the outside world is fine, but that he can be a little terror at home.

Socializing An Adult Dog

Sometimes an adult dog will be too set in his ways to change, particularly if your dog is in his golden years. However, most adult dogs can be socialized as long as you make it your top priority (along with training). If you aren't prepared to be very patient with your Shiba Inu adult, then it is best not to adopt an adult. Their headstrong nature makes it a lot of work, and you have to be willing to be patient. Before you can begin to socialize your dog, you need to make sure he already knows some basic commands and that you have him under control before any introductions are made.

Socializing an adult canine requires a lot of time, dedication, gentle training, and a firm approach. You may be lucky enough to get an adult that is already well socialized. However, that does not mean that you can

Photo Courtesy of
Brooke Steinbach

be entirely relaxed. The dog may have had a bad experience with a particular breed of dog that no one knows about.

1. Your dog should be adept at the following commands before you work on socialization:

    a. Sit

    b. Down

    c. Heel

    It could be helpful for your dog to know stay and lie down as well. If your dog can remain in one place based on your commands, then your dog is demonstrating self-control, something that will be very helpful for socialization because you can override an aggressive impulse by activating the listening mode. When you go outside, you will need to be very aware of your surroundings (your Shiba Inu is going to be very alert, so you cannot be on your phone or doing anything apart from looking at your surroundings), and be able to command your dog before another dog or person gets near.

2. Use a short leash on walks. At the first sign of aggression, you need to turn and walk in the opposite direction. Being aware of your surroundings will start to cue you into what your dog is reacting to so you can start training your dog not to react negatively.

3. Change direction if you notice that your Shiba Inu is not reacting well to a particular person or dog approaching you. Avoidance is a good short term solution until you know that yo ur dog is more accepting of the presence of these other dogs or people.

    If you aren't able to take a different direction, tell your dog to sit, then block your dog's view. This can prove to be very challenging as your dog will try to look around you. Engage in training to help force your dog to listen to you, taking his mind off what is coming toward him.

4. Ask friends with friendly dogs to visit you, then meet in an enclosed space. Having one or two friendly dogs interact with your dog can help your Shiba Inu to see that not all dogs are dangerous or need to be put in their place. Having the dogs walk around the area together without a lot of interaction can help your dog learn that other dogs are usually just interested in enjoying the outside, so there is no reason to try to bully them.

5. Get special treats just for walks. If your dog is very aggressive when walking, have him sit, and give him one of the special treats. Shiba Inu are food driven, so this could be a perfect way of distracting your dog from whatever is making him feel protective. At the first snarl

or sign of aggression, engage the training mentality and draw upon your dog's desire for those special treats. This method is slow, but it is reliable over time because your dog is learning that the appearance of strangers and other dogs means special treats, a positive experience, not a negative one. However, this does not train the dog to interact with those dogs. You can couple it with the 4th suggestion to get the best results.

If you have problems with your adult dog, consult a behaviorist or specialized trainer.

Dealing With Domination

Dominant dogs are much more likely to act with some level of aggression when someone tries to interact with them and the dog isn't interested. They are also more likely to try to get their own way, which means constantly testing the rules. It is incredibly unlikely that they will back down or submit when faced with a challenge, increasing the odds of a fight.

The following will help you better handle a dominant dog.

- The best way to deal with this is to remain firm and calm. If you start yelling or creating fear in your Shiba Inu, you are just giving him more reasons to be upset and stressed, which is exactly the opposite of what you want. Instead of these negative reactions, remove your dog from stressful situations.

- Do not use any kind of physical punishment to correct your dog. This encourages him to react physically, increasing the odds of him biting or lunging at others.

- Always monitor your dog's interactions with others, especially in the early days, so you can step in before the warning signs of aggression manifest as actions.

- Being consistent is absolutely essential to helping your Shiba Inu learn the rules. If you don't want your Shiba Inu to be protective of toys, you cannot let your dog growl when people get near the toys. If you don't want your Shiba Inu on the furniture, you can never let your Shiba Inu on the furniture. Any deviation from the rules is going to be seen as a weakness in you. Set the rules and then always stick to them. This will mean ensuring everyone in the family complies as well.

- Obedience classes are recommended. Chapter 12 provides a bit more information about when to begin classes.

- Have the appropriate equipment for your dog. If your dog has bitten someone in the past, you should have a basket muzzle to prevent further biting when you have visitors. If your dog shows any signs of aggression, a drag lead can be helpful for ensuring you keep your Shiba Inu under control on walks.

Taking a dominant dog to a dog park is a unique challenge, and it is as much about monitoring the other people and dogs as your own. Dog

Photo Courtesy of Marvin Forquer

parks can be a great place for your dog to socialize, but you need to vis-it a park where there are responsible people. You don't want to go to a place where the people spend more time socializing with each other and ignoring their dogs. This increases the odds of a fight.

If you do choose to go into the dog park, you will need to be con-stantly aware of your dog. You need to not only watch for signs of trou-ble with your dog, but you need to make sure that people aren't treating your dog in a way that is not acceptable. They may want to pet and play with your Shiba Inu because of how adorable your dog is. If your Shiba Inu isn't interested, you don't want people (particularly children) trying to play with him. You also don't want other people trying to "train" your Shiba Inu because that will not go well.

CHAPTER 12
Training Your Shiba Inu

"It is best to train your Shiba pup to obey and stay near you. The breed is known for taking off and running if the opportunity arises."

Jan Hill
Dark Knight Shibas

Shiba Inu are the kind of breed that is always able to learn something new, and if they are in the mood, it can be both fun and rewarding. If they aren't in the mood though, training will be exponentially difficult. This is a breed that has both energy and brains, so you have a lot of options in how you want to train your dog. Commands like roll over, speak, high five, and play dead will be about as easy for a Shiba Inu as most of the basic commands – as long as your Shiba Inu wants to learn. Take some time to check out all of the fun things that Shiba Inu can do. They may like to have things their way, but they also love to learn and they are incredibly adept learners.

The one thing to keep in mind is that you have to be patient. There is a reason why the Shiba Inu makes nearly every list of one of the most difficult breeds to train, and there are far more wrong ways to train them than right, considering how stubborn they are.

Photo Courtesy of Whitney Kono

Benefits Of Proper Training

In addition to making socialization and general excursions easier, training could be a way of saving your dog's life. Understanding commands will help to stop your dog from running into the street or from responding to provocations from other dogs (or from acting as the aggressor). As escape artists, this could also be a time saver in the event your dog gets away from you.

Photo Courtesy of Ashley Antill

Training is a great way to bond with your dog. It gives you dedicated time together and helps you to understand a puppy's developing personality and to learn what kinds of rewards will work best for other tasks, like socialization.

The most enjoyable benefit of having a solid foundation for training is being able to train your dog to do so much more. This is a dog that can join in with so many human activities, such as kayaking, hiking, and playing ball, you want to make sure your Shiba Inu is trained so that you can enjoy a full range of activities.

Choosing The Right Reward

"Training can be a challenge! Some Shibas are not food motivated, nor will work just for pets. They often do not make good obedience dogs, because they like to do things THEIR way."

CJ Strehle
JADE Shiba Inu

The right reward for a Shiba Inu will ultimately be love and affection. Treats are the easiest way of keying a puppy into the idea that performing tricks is a good behavior. Soon, though, you will need to switch to something that is a secondary reinforcer. Praise, additional playtime,

Photo Courtesy of
Karolina Bialkowska

and extra petting are all fantastic rewards for Shiba Inu, depending on your dog's current mood. Despite their occasional cold shoulder, they do love their people. They just aren't likely to trail around behind you like a lot of other dog breeds. Plopping down to watch a movie and letting your puppy sit with you is a great reward after an intense training session. Not only did your puppy learn, but you both now get to relax together.

If you would like your Shiba Inu to attach positive feedback with a sound, you can use a clicker. They are relatively inexpensive and will need to be used at the same time as you praise your puppy or dog. They are not necessary, but some trainers do use them. It is up to you if you want one more thing to carry while training and walking your puppy.

Name Recognition

Over time, many of us come up with multiple names for our dogs. Nicknames, joke names, and descriptions based on some of their ridiculous actions (it's why we love them) can all be used later. However, before you can train a dog, you have to make sure your dog understands his real name.

1. Get some treats and show one to your dog.
2. Say the dog's name, immediately say "Yes" (your dog should be looking at you when you speak), then give your dog a treat.
3. Wait 10 seconds, then show your dog a treat and repeat step 2.

Sessions shouldn't last longer than about five minutes because your dog will lose either focus or interest. Name recognition is something you can do several times over the day. After you have done this over five to ten sessions, the training will change a bit.

1. Wait until your dog isn't paying attention to you.
2. Call your dog. If the dog has a leash on, give it a gentle tug to get your dog's attention.
3. Say "Yes" and give the dog a treat when he looks at you.

During this time, do not speak your dog's name during corrections or for no real reason. This is because in the beginning, you need to get the dog to associate the name only with something very positive, like treats. This will more quickly program your dog to listen to you no matter what else is going on around him.

It is likely that your Shiba Inu will not require a lot of time before he recognizes his name.

Photo Courtesy of
Sophie Riggs

Essential Commands

There are five basic commands that all dogs should know. These commands are the basis for a happy and enjoyable relationship with your dog. By the time your puppy learns all five of the commands, it will be more obvious what the correlation between the words you say and the expected actions are. This will clue the dog in to understanding new words in terms of expectation and will make it much easier to train him on the more complex concepts.

Train your puppy to do the commands in the order they appear in this chapter. Sit is a basic command, and something all dogs already naturally do. Since dogs tend to sit often, it is the easiest one to teach. Teaching leave it and drop it is much more difficult, and it usually requires that the puppy fight an instinct or desire. Consider how much you give in to something you want to do when you know you shouldn't – that's pretty much what you are facing, but with a puppy. Quiet can be another difficult command as dogs (particularly puppies) tend to bark as a natural reaction to something. These two commands will take longer to teach, so you want to have the necessary tools already in place to increase your odds of success.

Here are some basic guidelines to follow during training.

- Include everyone in the home in the Shiba Inu training. The puppy must learn to listen to everyone in the household, and not just one or two people. A set training schedule may only involve a couple of people in the beginning, especially if you have children. There should always be an adult present for training, but including one child during training will help reinforce the idea that the puppy must listen to everyone in the house. It is also a good way for the parent to monitor the child's interaction with the puppy so that everyone plays in a way that is safe and follows the rules.

- To get started, select an area where you and your puppy have no other distractions, including noise. Leave your phone and other devices out of range so that you keep your attention on the puppy.

- Stay happy and excited about the training. Your puppy will pick up on your enthusiasm, and will focus better because of it.

- Be consistent and firm as you teach.

- Bring a special treat to the first few training sessions, such as pieces of chicken or small treats.

Sit

Start to teach sit when your puppy is around eight weeks old. Once you settle into your quiet training location:

1. Hold out a treat.
2. Move the treat over your puppy's head. This will make the puppy move back.
3. Say 'sit' as the puppy's haunches touch the floor.

Having a second person around to demonstrate this with your puppy will be helpful as they can sit to show what you mean.

Wait until your puppy starts to sit down and say sit as he or she sits. If your puppy finishes sitting down, give praise. Naturally, this will make your puppy incredibly excited and wiggly, so it may take a bit of time before he will want to sit again. When the time comes and the puppy starts to sit again, repeat the process.

It's going to take more than a couple of sessions for the puppy to fully connect your words with the actions. Commands are something completely new to your little companion. Once your puppy has demonstrated a mastery over sit, start teaching down.

Down

Repeat the same process to teach this command as you did for sit.

1. Tell your dog to sit.
2. Hold out the treat.
3. Lower the treat to the floor with your dog sniffing at it. Allow your pup to lick the treat, but if your dog stands up, start over.
4. Say down as the puppy's elbows touch the floor, then give praise while letting your puppy eat the treat.

Wait until the puppy starts to lie down, then say the word down. If the Shiba Inu finishes the action, offer your chosen reward.

It will probably take a little less time to teach this command.

Wait until your puppy has mastered down before moving on to stay.

Stay

Stay is a vital command to teach because it can keep your puppy from running across a street or from running at someone who is nervous or scared of dogs. It is important that your dog has mastered sit and down before you teach stay. Learning this command is going to be more difficult since it isn't something that your puppy does naturally. Be prepared for it to take a bit longer.

1. Tell your puppy to either sit or stay.

2. As you do this, place your hand in front of the puppy's face.

3. Wait until the puppy stops trying to lick your hand before you begin again.

4. When the puppy settles down, take a step away. If your puppy is not moving, say stay and give a treat and some praise.

Giving your puppy the reward indicates that the command is over, but you also need to indicate that the command is complete. The puppy has to learn to stay until you say it is okay to leave the spot. Once you give the okay to move, do not give treats. Come should not be used as the okay word as it is a command used for something else.

Repeat these steps, taking more steps further from the puppy after a successful command.

Once your puppy understands stay when you move away, start training to stay even if you are not moving. Extend the amount of time required for the puppy to stay in one spot so that he understands that stay ends with the okay command.

When you feel that your puppy has stay mastered, start to train the puppy to come.

Come

This is a command you can't teach until the puppy has learned the previous commands. Before you start the training session, decide if you want to use come or come here for the command. Be consistent in the words you use.

This command is important for the same reason as the previous one. If you are around people who are nervous around dogs, or encounter a wild animal or other distraction, this command can snap your puppy's attention back to you.

1. Leash the puppy.

2. Tell the puppy to stay.

3. Move away from the puppy.

4. Say the command you will use for come and give a gentle tug on the leash toward you.

Repeat these steps, building a larger distance between you and the puppy. Once the puppy seems to understand it, remove the leash and start at a close distance. If your puppy doesn't seem to understand the command, give some visual clues about what you want. For example, you can pat your leg or snap your fingers. As soon as your puppy comes running over to you, offer a reward.

Off

Although Shiba Inu are small, it's important to train your dog to get down or off something. This is not the same as teaching your dog not to jump on people (Chapter 9). This command is specifically to get your dog off furniture, off counters, and your lap (Shiba Inu are not always the lap dogs they seem to think they are).

This is training that you will need to be prepared to do on the fly because you are training your dog to stop an action. This means you have to react to that undesirable action. Having treats on hand will be essential when you see your dog getting up on things you don't want him to be on.

1. Wait for your dog to put his paws on something that you don't want him on.
2. Say "Off" and lure him away with a treat that you keep just out of his reach.
3. Say "Yes" and give him a treat as soon as his paws are off the surface.

Repeat this every time you see the behavior. It will likely take at least half a dozen times before your dog understands he should not perform the action anymore. Over time, switch from treats to praise or playing with a toy.

Leave It

This is a difficult training command, but you need to teach your dog leave it for when you are out on a walk and want him to ignore other people or dogs.

1. Let your dog see that you have treats in your hand, then close it. Your fist should be close enough for your dog to sniff the treat.
2. Say "Leave it" when your dog starts to sniff your hand.
3. Say "Yes" and give your dog a treat when he turns his head away from the treats. Initially, this will probably take a while as your dog will want those treats. Don't continue to say "Leave it" as your dog should not be learning that you will give a command more than once. You want him to learn that he must do what you say the first time you say

it. You will need to coax your dog to respond quickly, which is why treats are recommended in the beginning. If a minute or more passes after giving the command, you can then issue it again, but make sure your canine is focused on you and not distracted.

These sessions should only last about five minutes and it will take your dog some time to learn, as you are teaching him to ignore something he does naturally. When he starts to understand and looks away when you say leave it without spending much time sniffing, you can move on to more advanced versions of the training.

1. Leave your hand open so that your dog can see the treats.

2. Say "Leave it" when your dog starts to show interest (this will probably be almost immediately, especially since you won't have your hand closed, so be prepared).

   a. Close your fist if your dog continues to sniff or gets near the treats in your hand.

   b. Give your dog a treat from your other hand if he stops.

Repeat these steps until your dog finally stops trying to sniff the treats. When your dog seems to have this down, move on to the most difficult version of this command.

1. Place treats on the ground, or let your dog see you hide them, and stay close to those treats.

2. Say "Leave it" when your dog starts to show interest in sniffing the treats.

   a. Place a hand over the treats if he doesn't listen.

   b. Give him a treat from your hand if your dog does listen.

From here, you can start training while standing further from the treat with your dog leashed so you can stop him if needed. Then start to use other things that your dog loves, such as a favorite toy or another tempting treat that you don't usually give.

Drop It

This is going to be one of the most difficult commands you will teach your puppy because it goes against both your puppy's instincts and interests. Your puppy wants to keep whatever he has, so you are going to have to offer him something better instead. It is essential to teach the command early though, as your Shiba Inu is going to be very destructive in the early days. Furthermore, this command could save your pooch's

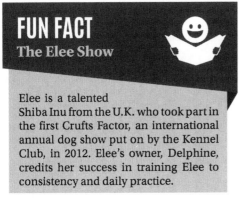

life. He is likely to lunge at things that look like food when you are out for a walk and this command will get him to drop anything potentially hazardous that he picks up.

Start with a toy and a treat, or a large treat that your dog cannot eat in a matter of seconds, such as a raw hide. Make sure the treat you have is one that your puppy does not get very often so that there is motivation to drop the toy or big treat.

1. Give your puppy the toy or large treat. If you want to use a clicker too, pair it with the exciting treat that you will use to help convince your puppy to drop the treat.

2. Show your puppy the exciting treat.

3. Say Drop it and when he drops the treat or toy, tell him good and hand over the exciting treat while picking up the dropped treat or toy.

4. Repeat this immediately after your puppy finishes the exciting treat.

You will need to keep reinforcing this command for months after it is learned because it is not a natural reaction. You should also start using food that your dog finds almost irresistible. This is one of those rare times when you must use a treat because your puppy needs something to convince him to drop a cherished toy, or more importantly, food that he shouldn't be eating.

Quiet

Shiba Inu aren't considered excessive barkers, but there is no guarantee that yours won't be vocal. Initially, you can use treats sparingly to reinforce quiet if your pup enjoys making noise. If your puppy barks with no obvious reason, tell him to be quiet and place a treat nearby. It is almost guaranteed that the dog will fall silent to sniff the treat, in which case, say good dog or good quiet. It will not take too long for your puppy to understand that quiet means no barking.

Where To Go From Here

"Shibas can be very easy to train, as they are intuitive and keen. However, they do not do anything to please us, only themselves. They seldom do anything just for praise; they need motivation. Fortunately, most are toy or food motivated, so that works well. The dogs who don't care about toys or food can be very difficult - they know what it is 'we' want, but they just don't see why they should do it."

Susan Norris-Jones
SunJo Shiba Inu & Japanese Chin

This is a breed that can very much benefit from obedience training. Because they are so headstrong, obedience training is as much about training you in how to react to stubbornness as it is about training your dog to be obedient. It also gives your Shiba Inu a chance to socialize. It is a safe environment for your pup to learn about other dogs because there is a lot of attention being given to all of the dogs. It is a safe environment and a great experience for you to both learn.

Puppy Classes

Puppies can begin to go to puppy school as early as 6 weeks. This is the beginning of obedience training, but you will need to be careful about their interactions with other dogs until your puppy has completed his vaccinations. Talk with your vet about when is a good time to begin, or at least a safe time. Your vet may be able to recommend good puppy training classes in your area.

The primary purpose of these classes is socialization, which is really important for a breed like the Shiba Inu. Studies have shown that a third of puppies have minimal exposure to new people and dogs during the first 20 weeks of their life, which can make the outside world scarier. The puppy classes give you and your puppy a chance to learn how to meet and greet other people and dogs in a strictly controlled environment. Dogs who attend these classes are much friendlier and are less stressed about things like large trucks, loud noises, and visitors. They are also less likely to be nervous or suffer from separation anxiety.

It is also good training for you. In the same studies, people were better able to react appropriately when a puppy was disobedient or misbehaved, something that is absolutely essential when training a Shiba Inu.

It teaches you how to train your puppy and how to deal with the emerging headstrong nature of your dog.

Many classes will help you with some of the basic commands, like sit and down. Look for a class that also focuses on socialization so that your puppy can get the most out of the class.

Obedience Training

After your puppy graduates from puppy school and understands most of the basics commands, you can switch to obedience classes. They are more difficult, but it shouldn't be that much of a challenge for a Shiba Inu. Some trainers offer at home obedience training, but it is best to find a class so that your dog can continue socialization as a part of training. If your puppy attends puppy classes, they can provide you with the next classes that they recommend. Dogs of nearly any age can attend obedience training classes, though your dog should be old enough to listen (this is why there are puppy classes – dogs who are 20 weeks old or less are a different kind of training problem).

Obedience training usually includes the following:

- Teaching or reinforcing basic commands, like sit, stay, come, and down.

- How to walk without pulling on the leash.

- How to properly greet people and dogs, including not jumping on them.

Obedience school is as much about training you as training your dog. It helps you learn how to train while getting your dog through basic commands and how to behave for basic attacks, like greetings and walking. Classes usually last between 7 and 10 weeks.

Ask your vet for recommendations. If your vet doesn't have any recommendations, take time to thoroughly research your options. Look at the following details when evaluating trainers:

- Are they certified, particularly the CPDT-KA certification.

- How many years have they been training dogs?

- Do they have experiences with Shiba Inu?

- Can you participate in the training? If the answer is no, do not use this trainer. You have to be a part of your dog's training because the trainer is not going to be around most of your dog's life. He has to learn to listen to you.

Obedience training does not help with serious behavioral issues. If your dog has anxiety, depression, or other serious behavioral issues, you need to hire a trainer to help your dog work through those issues. Do your research to make sure your selected trainer is an expert, preferably with experience with intelligent, strong-willed dogs. If possible, find someone who has experience dealing with Shiba Inu.

Once your Shiba Inu has the basic commands down and has done well in obedience training, you can start to do other more enjoyable training. As long as your Shiba Inu did well in the classes, you should not need a trainer because your dog will listen to you. With a foundation for commands and a more active interest in learning more, this could be a great foundation for doing more – as long as your Shiba Inu is interested. By this point, you should be able to tell if your dog is interested, and you will definitely have more of an idea if you want to pursue more difficult training given your dog's personality.

CHAPTER 13
Nutrition

"As an Asian breed, they do not have a history with beef or grains, which require specific digestive enzymes. Poultry, fish, game are good protein sources, while rice is the best tolerated grain."

Susan Norris-Jones
SunJo Shiba Inu & Japanese Chin

Over the past few years, people have been allowing their Shiba Inu to become too big for their small frames because of the popularity of Cody, an obese Shiba Inu. People thought that the problems he was having were "cute," which is cruel because that panting and the look on the dog's face is indicative of pain, not happiness. You have to be careful with your Shiba Inu to ensure this does not happen to him. While

they aren't prone to overeating like some other breeds, that doesn't mean they won't do it.

It is surprisingly easy to keep this breed healthy though. You just have to be aware of what you are feeding your Shiba Inu and make sure your dog is getting adequate exercise every day. Given their size, this is easy to do, but it does requires planning before your puppy or dog arrives.

Why A Healthy Diet Is Important

Since Shiba Inu usually adjust their exercise needs to match the family's level of exercise, you are going to need to adjust the diet to match the amount of exercise your dog will get regularly. This is a unique problem for Shiba Inu parents, so you will need to be careful of any decline in activity to make sure you aren't overfeeding your dog. If you have a very busy schedule, it will be entirely too easy to have substantial lapses in activity levels while you are home. Your Shiba Inu isn't going to understand your schedule changes, just the fact that there is usually a certain amount of food going into his mouth, regardless of his activity level. This means he is likely to gain weight when you keep the calories the same while reducing the activities.

You need to be aware of roughly how many calories your dog eats a day, including treats. Be aware of your dog's weight so you can see when he is putting on pounds. This will key you in to when you should adjust how much food your Shiba Inu eats a day, or change his food to something with more nutritional value, but fewer calories.

Always talk with your vet if you have concerns about your Shiba Inu's weight. You can also establish regular weight checks at home because they fit on home scales.

Canine Nutrition

The dietary needs of a dog are significantly different than a human's needs. People are more omnivorous than dogs, meaning they require a wider range of nutrients to be healthy. Canines are largely carnivorous, and protein is a significant dietary requirement. However, they need more than just protein to be healthy.

The following table provides the primary nutritional requirements for dogs.

Nutrient	Sources	Puppy	Adult
Protein	Meat, eggs, soybeans, corn, wheat, peanut butter	22.0% of diet	18.0% of diet
Fats	Fish oil, flaxseed oil, canola oil, pork fat, poultry fat, safflower oil, sunflower oil, soybean oil	8.0 to 15.0% of diet	5.0 to 15.0% of diet
Calcium	Dairy, animal organ tissue, meats, legumes (typically beans)	1.0% of diet	0.6% of diet
Phosphorus	Meat and pet supplements	0.8% of diet	0.5% of diet
Sodium	Meat, eggs	0.3% of diet	0.06% of diet

The following are the remaining nutrients dogs require, all of them less than 1% of the puppy or adult diet:

- Arginine
- Histidine
- Isoleucine
- Leucine
- Lysine
- Methionine + cystine
- Phenylalanine + tyrosine
- Threonine
- Tryptophan
- Valine
- Chloride

Photo Courtesy of Whitney Kono

Since so many human foods contain preservatives and salt, it is best to avoid giving your dog human foods with a lot of sodium.

Water is also absolutely essential to keeping your dog healthy. There should always be water in your dog's water bowl, so make a habit of checking it several times a day so that your dog does not get dehydrated.

Proteins And Amino Acids

As carnivores, protein is one of the most important nutrients in a healthy dog's diet (although they should not eat meat nearly as exclusively as their close wolf relatives; their diets and needs have changed significantly since they became companions to humans). Proteins contain the necessary amino acids for your dog to produce glucose, which is essential for giving your dog energy.

A lack of protein in your dog's diet will result in him being lethargic. His coat may start to look dull and he is likely to lose weight. Conversely, if your dog gets too much protein, your dog's body will store the excess protein as fat, meaning he will gain weight.

Meat is typically the best source of protein, and it is recommended since a dog's dietary needs are significantly different from a human's needs. However, it is possible for a dog to have a vegetarian diet as long as you ensure that your dog gets the necessary protein through other sources, and you will include supplemental vitamin D in his food. If you plan to feed your dog a vegetarian diet, talk to your vet first. It is incredibly difficult to ensure that a carnivore gets adequate protein with a vegetarian diet, especially puppies, so you will need to dedicate a lot of time to research and discussion with nutrition experts to ensure that your dog is getting the necessary proteins for his needs.

Fat And Fatty Acids

Most of the fats that your dog needs also come from meat, though seed oils can provide a lot of the necessary healthy fats too, with peanut butter being one of the most common sources. Fats are broken down into fatty acids, which your dog needs for fat-soluble vitamins that help with regular cell functions. Perhaps the most obvious benefit of fats and fatty acids is in your dog's coat, which will look and feel much healthier when your dog is getting the right nutrients.

There are a number of potential health issues if your dog does not get adequate fats in his daily diet.

- His coat will look less healthy.
- His skin may be dry and itchy.

Photo Courtesy of
Helena Miltiadous

- His immune system could be compromised, making it easier for your dog to get sick.

- He may have an increased risk of heart disease.

The primary concern if your dog gets too much fat is that he will gain weight and become obese, leading to additional health problems. For breeds that are predisposed to heart problems, you need to be particularly careful to ensure your dog gets the right amount of fats in his diet. An estimated 18% of Shiba Inu have heart problems.

Carbohydrates And Cooked Foods

Dogs have been living with humans for millennia, so their dietary needs have evolved like our own. They are able to eat foods with carbohydrates to supplement the energy typically provided by proteins and fats. If you cook up grains (such as barley, corn, rice, and wheat) prior to feeding them to your dog, it will be easier for your dog to digest those complex carbohydrates. This is something to keep in mind when considering what type of food you will feed your dog as you want to get a kibble (dry dog food) that uses meat instead of grains; while your dog can digest food with grains, he won't get as much of the nutritional value as he would from food that has real meat.

Different Dietary Requirements For Different Life Stages

Different stages of a dog's life have different nutritional needs:
- Puppies
- Adults
- Senior dogs

Puppy Food

Dog food manufacturers produce a completely different type of food for puppies for a very good reason – their nutritional needs are much different than their adult counterparts. During roughly the first 12 months of their lives their bodies are growing. To be healthy, they need more calories and have different nutritional needs to promote that growth.

Adult Dog Food

The primary difference between puppy food and adult dog food is that puppy food is higher in calories and nutrients that promote growth. Dog food producers reduce these nutrients in food made for adult dogs as they no longer need to sustain growth. As a general rule, when a dog reaches about 90% of his predicted adult size, you should switch to adult dog food.

The size of your dog is key in determining how much to feed him. The following table is a general recommendation on how much to feed your adult Shiba Inu a day. Initially, you may want to focus on the calories as you try to find the right balance for your dog.

Dog Size	Calories
10 lbs.	420 during hot months 630 during cold months
20 lbs.	700 during hot months 1,050 during cold months

Notice that most Shiba Inu don't need 1,000 calories a day most of the year. This is not a lot of food, so you need to be very aware of how many calories you are giving your dog to ensure your dog does not become overweight. This scale is for a dog's ideal weight range. If your dog is overweight or obese, ask your vet about how much you should be feeding your dog per day.

Also keep mind that these recommendations are per day, and not per meal. Whether you feed him once a day or several times per day, make sure that you carefully measure out how much food you give so that you do not exceed the daily recommendation.

If you plan to add wet food, pay attention to the total calorie intake and adjust how much you feed your dog between the kibble and wet food. In other words, the total calories in the kibble and wet food should balance out so as not to exceed your dog's needs.

The same is true if you give your dog a lot of treats over the course of the day. You should factor treat calorie counts into how much you feed your dog at mealtimes.

If you plan to feed your dog homemade food, you will need to learn more about nutrition, and you will need to pay close attention to calories, and not cup measurements.

Senior Dog Food

Like older people, senior dogs aren't capable of being as active as they were in their younger days. This is just a rough guideline though. If you notice your dog slowing down or see that your dog isn't able to take longer walks because of joint pain or a lack of stamina, that is a good sign that your dog is entering his senior years. Consult with your vet when you think it is time to change the type of food you give your dog.

The primary difference between adult and senior dog food is that senior dog food has less fat and more antioxidants to help fight weight gain. Senior dogs also need more protein, which will probably make your dog happy because that usually means more meat and meat flavors. Protein helps to maintain your dog's aging muscles. He should be eating less phosphorous during his golden years to avoid the risk of your dog developing hyperphosphatemia. This is a condition where dogs have excessive amounts of phosphate in their blood stream, and older dogs are at greater risk of developing it.

Senior dog food has the right amount of calories for the reduced activity, so you shouldn't need to adjust how much food you give your dog, unless you notice that he is putting on weight. Consult your vet before you adjust the amount of food or if you notice that your dog is putting on weight. This could be a sign of a senior dog ailment.

Your Dog's Meal Options

You have three primary choices for what to feed your dog, or you can use a combination of the three, depending on your situation and your dog's specific needs:

- Commercial foods
- Raw diet
- Homemade diet

Commercial Food

Make sure that you are buying the best dog food that you can afford. Take the time to research each of your options, particularly the nutritional value of the food, and make this an annual task. You want to make sure that the food you are giving your dog is quality food. Always account for your dog's size, energy levels, and age. Your puppy may not need puppy food as long as other breeds and dog food for seniors may not be the best option for your own senior Shiba Inu.

Barkspace provides several great articles about which commercial dog foods are good for Shiba Inu. Since new foods frequently come on the market, check back occasionally to see if there are newer, better foods available. Since you have to be careful of your Shiba Inu's weight, it is well worth verifying that you are giving him the best food available.

If you aren't sure about which brand of food is best, talk with the breeder about what foods they recommend. You can ask your vet, though odds are most of them have not worked with many Shiba Inu and haven't formed an opinion yet. Breeders are really the best guides for you here, as they are experts in the breed.

Photo Courtesy of
Pervie Villareal

Some dogs may be picky, and they can certainly get tired of having the same food repeatedly. Just as you switch up your meals, you can change what your Shiba Inu eats. While you shouldn't frequently change the brand of food, you can get foods that have different flavors. You can also change the taste by adding a bit of wet (canned) food. This is an easy change to make, giving your dog a different canned food (usually just about 1/4 to 1/3 of the can for a meal, depending on your dog's size) with each meal.

For more details on commercial options, check out Dog Food Advisor. They provide reviews on the different brands, as well as providing information on recalls and contamination issues.

Commercial Dry Food

Dry dog food often comes in bags, and it is what the vast majority of people feed their dogs. Given their size, you won't need the large bags of dog food unless you don't want to purchase it for a very long time.

Pros of dry dog food:
- Convenience
- Variety
- Availability
- Affordability
- Manufacturers follow nutritional recommendations (not all of them follow this, so do your brand research before you buy)
- Specially formulated for different canine life stages
- Can be used for training
- Easy to store

Cons of dry dog food:
- Requires research to ensure you don't buy doggie junk food
- Packaging is not always honest
- Recalls for food contamination
- Loose FDA nutritional regulations
- Low quality food may have questionable ingredients

The convenience and ease on your budget means that you are almost certainly going to buy kibble for your dog. This is perfectly fine, and most dogs will be more than happy to eat kibble. Just know what brand you are currently feeding your dog, and pay attention to kibble recalls to ensure you stop feeding your dog that particular food if necessary.

Commercial Wet Food

Most dogs prefer wet dog food to kibble, but it is also more expensive. Wet dog food can be purchased in larger packs that can be very easy to store.

Pros of wet dog food:

- Helps keep dogs hydrated
- Has a richer scent and flavor
- Easier to eat for dogs with dental problems (particularly those missing teeth) or if a dog has been ill
- Convenient and easy to serve
- Unopened, it can last between 1 and 3 years
- Balanced based on current pet nutrition recommendations

Cons of wet dog food:

- Dog bowls must be washed after every meal
- Can soften bowel movements
- Can be messier than kibble
- Once opened, it has a very short shelf life, and should be covered and refrigerated
- More expensive than dry dog food, and comes in small quantities
- Packaging is not always honest
- Recalls for food contamination
- Loose FDA regulations

FURTHER READING
Shiba in Folklore

Jojofu is a children's book that depicts a Shiba-like hunting dog named Jojofu who protects his master, Takumi, during a hunting trip. This book is a retelling of a medieval Japanese folktale and is geared towards children ages 5-7. It was published by Harper Collins in 1996 and illustrated by Yoriko Ito.

Like dry dog food, wet dog food is convenient, and picky dogs are much more likely to eat it than kibble. When your dog gets sick, it is best to use wet dog food to ensure that he is eating so that he gets the necessary nutrition he needs each day. It may be a bit harder to switch back to kibble once he is healthy, but you can always continue to add a little wet food to make each meal more appetizing to your dog.

Raw Diet

"I feed my Shibas a Raw diet, as I would for any dog. I think they do well, and live longer given raw, appropriate food. But I also know many people feed dry foods to their Shibas, and they also live long healthy lives."

CJ Strehle
JADE Shiba Inu

For dogs like the Shiba Inu that have food allergies, raw diets can help to keep your dog from having an allergic reaction to wheat and processed foods. Raw diets are heavy in raw meats, bones, vegetables, and specific supplements. Some of the benefits to a raw diet include:

- Improves your dog's coat and skin
- Improves immune system
- Improves health (as a result of better digestion)
- Increases energy
- Increases muscle mass

Raw diets are meant to give your dog the kind of food he ate before being domesticated. It means giving your dog uncooked meats, whole (uncooked) bones, and a bit of dairy. It doesn't include any processed food of any kind – not even food cooked in your kitchen.

There are potential risks to this diet. Dogs have been domesticated for millennia, and their digestive system has evolved as they have. Trying to force them back on the kind of diet they used to eat does not always work as intended because they may not be able to fully digest it anymore. There are also a lot of risks with feeding dogs uncooked meals, particularly if the food has been contaminated. Things like bacteria pose a serious risk and can be transferred to you if your dog gets sick. Many medical professionals also warn about the dangers of giving dogs bones, even if they are uncooked. Bones can splinter in your dog's mouth, puncturing the esophagus or stomach.

The Canine Journal provides a lot of information about the raw diet, including how to transition your current dog to this diet and different recipes for your dog.

Homemade Diet

If you regularly make your own food (from scratch, not with a microwave or boxed meal), it really doesn't take that much more time to provide an equally healthy meal for your companion.

Read through Chapter 4 to make sure that you never give your Shiba Inu foods that could be harmful or deadly to him. Keeping in mind the foods that your Shiba Inu absolutely should not eat, you can mix some of the food you make for yourself into your Shiba Inu's meal. Just make sure to add a bit more of what your Shiba Inu needs to the puppy's food bowl. Although you and your Shiba Inu have distinctly different dietary needs, you can tailor your foods to include nutrients that your dog needs.

Do not feed your Shiba Inu from your plate. Split the food, placing your dog's meal into a bowl so that your canine understands that your food is just for you. The best home cooked meals should be planned in advance so that your Shiba Inu is getting the right nutritional balance.

Typically, 50% of your dog's food should be animal protein (fish, poultry, and organ meats). About 25% should be full of complex carbohydrates. The remaining 25% should be from fruits and vegetables, particularly foods like pumpkin, apples, bananas, and green beans. These provide additional flavor that your Shiba Inu will probably love while making him feel full faster, so that the chance of overeating is reduced.

The following are a few sites you can use to learn to make meals for canines. Some of them are not Shiba Inu specific, so if you have more than one dog, these meals can be made for all of your furry canine friends:

- Dogsaholic - dogsaholic.com
- Life with Dogs - lifewithdogs.tv
- My First Shiba - myfirstshiba.com
- Northwest Shibas - northwestshibas.com/fido-recipes

Scheduling Meals

Working dogs expect a schedule – and they expect that food will also be provided on a set schedule, no matter what else is thrown off schedule. Your Shiba Inu may be independent, but he will likely expect you to stick to a schedule, and that definitely includes meal times. This is a breed that will have no problem with letting you know you are late with the food. If treats and snacks are something you establish as normal early on, your dog will believe that treats are also a part of the routine and will expect them.

Food Allergies And Intolerance

"If they start biting their feet or have diarrhea, that can mean they could have a food allergy."

Jan Hill
Dark Knight Shibas

Whenever you start your dog on a new type of dog food (even if it is the same brand that your dog is accustomed to, but a different flavor), you need to monitor him as he becomes accustomed to it. Shiba Inu are prone to numerous types of allergies, including food allergies. Whenever you change your dog's diet, you have to monitor for any indications that your pup is having an allergic reaction.

Food allergies in dogs tend to manifest themselves as hot spots, which are similar to rashes in humans. Your dog may start scratching or chewing specific spots on his body. His fur could start falling out around those spots.

Some dogs don't have a single hot spot, but the allergy shows up on their entire coat. If your Shiba Inu seems to be shedding more fur than normal, take your dog to the vet to have him checked for food allergies.

Shiba Inu don't usually have sensitive stomachs, but occasionally a poor pup does have some digestive issues. Sticking to a grain free diet can help ensure that your Shiba Inu is getting the right nutrition without suffering from food intolerance. If you do give your dog something that his stomach cannot handle, it will probably be obvious when he is unable to hold his bowels. If he is already housetrained, he will probably either pant at you or whimper to let you know that he needs to go outside. Get him outside as quickly as you can so that he does not have an accident. Depending on the dog, flatulence could be an indication of a food intolerance.

Since the symptoms of food allergies and intolerances can be similar to a dog's reaction to nutritional deficiencies (particularly a lack of fats in a dog's diet), you should visit your vet if you notice any problems with your dog's coat or skin.

CHAPTER 14
Active Or Lounger – Your Choice

Photo Courtesy of
Diane Leighton

Even though they are highly independent dogs, Shiba Inu are flex-ible. For people who prefer to be at home, they can fit right in and lounge around. For families that love to go out and be active, Shiba Inu can be just as energetic as teenagers. Their independence does not mean that they don't want to be with the family, it just means that they aren't going to cling to you. They love being with their people and pack, and they definitely want to get in on whatever fun you are having.

You will need to make sure that your Shiba Inu gets at least a 45 min-ute to an hour walk every day (and at least one shorter walk). They can also be tired out through more strenuous training. Of course, the differ-ent age groups have different exercise needs: puppies (Chapter 9) and senior dogs (Chapter 18) will not have the stamina for such long walks.

Given his intelligence and the risk of him getting bored, you want to keep your Shiba Inu either happily occupied or tired. This can be a unique challenge since your dog may not always be in the mood to do what you want to do. Though Shiba Inu may be very individualistic, they love to play with their people most of the time. The more options you give your Shiba Inu, the easier it will be to keep your pup out of trouble. On days when the weather makes it difficult to exercise, you can fall back on training or other fun indoor activities to expend some of that energy.

Exercise – The Activity Needs

"When young, Shiba puppies need a lot of rest and quiet times. They are not great exercisers until 4-5 months old. Once old enough, they will often do what is called the Shiba 500....racing around the yard or home to wear off energy. When full grown, Shibas need a long walk 2-3 times a week, or time to run around the yard daily to keep their minds bright and not destructive."

CJ Strehle
JADE Shiba Inu

Bringing a Shiba Inu into your home means you are agreeing to daily exercise, even when he is still a puppy. Dogs don't want to misbehave, but if they are bored, mischief is inevitable. Fortunately, their size makes exercising enough pretty easy, so when you finally leave your dog home alone, it's unlikely that your furniture or other things will be shredded in your absence.

Since weight problems are directly related to a lack of exercise, if your dog is gaining weight, that could be a sign that he isn't getting enough time moving about. Fortunately, it's easy to correct that; you have a lot of options for how to make sure your dog gets enough of a workout – it is much easier (and healthier for your friend) to do more with your dog than to just measure calories. You can even build a Shiba Inu's stamina up to the point of jogging several miles a day, and your dog will love it.

FUN FACT
Shiba Mari the YouTube Star

Mari, a Shiba Inu, and her owner, known as "Inosemarine," have developed a large following on Japanese YouTube for their comedic interactions. Mari and her owner have filmed their own cooking series, called "Cooking with Mari," as their take on the Japanese YouTube series "Cooking with Dog," as well as released a DVD! One of their most popular series depicts Mari shunning her owner's requests for kisses in hilarious ways.

A Wide Activity Range

Their appearance and inquisitive personality makes Shiba Inu a popular breed. Easily the most popular activity with this breed is hiking because they love to explore new places. The more different activities that you do with your dog, the happier you will both be.

Hiking

Most Shiba Inu thoroughly enjoy going out and exploring new areas. Despite their small stature, Shiba Inu can hike up to 10 miles in a day. They will be more than happy to join you on these hikes, so it will not be a fight to try to convince them it will be fun. After a trip out of doors, your Shiba Inu will be more than happy to just curl up for the rest of the day and lounge.

For hikes, make sure to take a water bowl and first aid kit. Make sure your Shiba Inu is current on flea and tick treatments too. He will need a couple of months' worth of treatments prior to outdoor excursions. Also,

Photo Courtesy of
Gabe & Natty Hynes

verify that dogs are allowed in the areas that you plan to explore. Take a map with you so that you don't get lost – your Shiba Inu is going to want to go all over the place, Make sure to keep your Shiba Inu on the leash while you explore. The prey drive will be at its strongest out on a hike, so you need to have your canine leashed to keep him safe.

Jogging

"Running and jogging are great exercises that a Shiba will thrive on. Or, at least a long brisk walk with active, interactive play time."

Jeffrey Kellen
JAK Kennel

Despite their size, Shiba Inu make fantastic jogging partners, and they can go a lot further than most other small and medium sized dogs. On days when you have to go to work, a jog in the morning is the perfect way to make sure your Shiba Inu is too tired to be bored while you are out.

You will need to start slow after consulting with your vet about taking your canine for a jog. It is recommended that you jog on dirt or soft ground because concrete and asphalt are much harder on leg joints. If you do have to jog on harder surfaces, give your canine's paws some time to acclimate to the surface. You may want to get some special lotions to use on those cute little pads after jogs on hard surfaces.

Plan to jog for about 10 minutes at least a few times. It is not a natural action to jog on a leash, so your dog is going to have to get used to it first, especially learning not to bite the leash as it is likely to hit your dog during the jog. During those 10 minutes switch between a minute of jogging, and a minute of walking. This will help your dog learn what you are trying to do. Over time, you will be able to start jogging more than walking. Once you can jog a full mile without walking, you will be able to start going a little further until you reach a few miles.

Be very careful about jogging when it gets warm, and do not jog when it is hot. Shiba Inu have a double coat, which will make them heat up a lot faster than you will. They sweat by panting, as all dogs do, and that is not as efficient with a thick coat of fur. If you do jog when it is warm, make sure to take water for your Shiba Inu, and let your dog drink at least every mile.

You need to have a very sturdy leash or halter to jog with your Shiba Inu as he will chase any small animals he sees. You don't want him to dislocate your shoulder, break the leash, or hurt himself if he veers to try to chase little animals.

Don't get upset if your dog wants to stop and sniff. That's just as exciting for him as simply jogging. If you want to jog without interruption, you may not want to jog with your Shiba Inu, at least not in the beginning.

Kayaking And Paddle Boarding

There aren't many dogs that are able to do this, but the Shiba Inu is the perfect dog for going out on the water with you and just enjoying the ride. He will love doing this just as much as you do, and his excitement at something so special will definitely make you feel incredible. Shiba Inu aren't known for being particularly adept swimmers, but they will be per-

Photo Courtesy of Alayne Levine

Photo Courtesy of
Helena Miltiadous

fectly happy to sit in the kayak or on the paddle board while you do all of the work.

You will need a floatation vest for your Shiba Inu, even if you are going out on still water. Since most kayaking and paddle boarding are done on much choppier water, you need to make sure that your little guy is safe. It is also possible that you will capsize, so you want to make sure that your Shiba Inu stays above water as you struggle to get the vessel turned upright.

You can practice for this by letting your dog explore the kayak or paddle board at home. Put it out in the yard or driveway and let him sniff it. Make sure that your dog does not urinate on the vessel. Your pup may also be too afraid to get into the vessel. Reassure him with positive words and tone as you carry him and get into or onto the vessel. Let your dog get used to this while on land so it won't be too much to take in when you reach the water.

Be prepared for the first few times to be incredibly exciting, so your dog will probably not sit still for it. This means you will need to go somewhere with calm water so that your dog can get accustomed to the feel.

Agility Training

Better known as obstacle courses, agility training is a great way to keep your adult dog running and happy. You get to guide your dog through the course, helping not only to build your bond, but also to give your dog a chance to feel more comfortable when he is outside the home, or at least learn that he doesn't need to try to dominate everyone in the area. Since you are the one in control, and your dog will likely be confused in the beginning, be prepared to look a bit silly at first. The point is to have fun and to keep your dog engaged, so getting and keeping his attention is key to being successful.

Two to three hours of dedicated time are recommended a week, with one of those hours going to a weekly class. The more you can train at home, the better your dog will do in this sport.

Photo Courtesy of Buck Motzko

Playtime! And More Playtime!

"Chasing a ball or toy is a good way to burn off that energy, being sure that the footing is good (i.e. grass or gravel, not slippery). Playing time at same time every day is a good way to create a routine. Practice 'recall' by using a treat during playtime, but don't stop playing. That way puppy won't associate being called with an end to the fun."

Susan Norris-Jones
SunJo Shiba Inu & Japanese Chin

Just because there is inclement weather doesn't mean that your dog's energy levels will be any lower, or that boredom won't set in, so you'll need to plan to keep your dog's exercise schedule consistent, even when you are stuck inside the house. Of course, if you can put your dog out to play in the snow in a backyard, that will be fantastic as he can tire himself out in his excitement. During rain and heat, you need to find the right activities to tire your canine without going outside for extended periods of time. Here are some alternatives to help expend your Shiba Inu's energy.

1. Let your Shiba Inu chase a laser pointer. This works for some Shiba Inu, but not all. If your dog seems interested, this can keep him happily occupied for as long as you want to play or until he gets bored.

2. Hide and seek is a game you can play once your dog knows about proper behavior in the home, whether you have him find you or a favorite toy you've hidden.

3. Puzzle toys are a great way to get your dog to move around without you having to do much. Many of the games come with treats, and knowing Shiba Inu, it won't be long before your dog figures out how to get the food out of the toy, so make sure you rotate various puzzles at playtime. Use these kinds of toys sparingly to avoid piling on the extra calories.

4. Shiba Inu love to play with a number of different balls, from rubber balls to football/soccer balls. Have a different set around just for you and your dog to play whatever game your Shiba Inu is interested in playing. If he wants to play fetch, use a small ball. If he wants to play with something bigger, make adjustments. Let your Shiba Inu decide what he is in the mood to do, then you can both have fun.

CHAPTER 15
Grooming – Productive Bonding

"Shibas shed a couple of times per year, so need to be brushed often to keep hair from your furniture and clothes. Their coat does not need trimming, as it is short and fluffy, but does not get matted or tangled. Their correct harsh outer coat sheds dirt and rain, and undercoat keeps them warm in the cold, so they can be outside for a walk or a run around the yard, without using a coat or sweater."

CJ Strehle
JADE Shiba Inu

That eye-catching double coat definitely requires more work than grooming a lot of small to medium-sized dogs, but Shiba Inu also are prolific self-cleaners, like cats. Some of them may take offense to you feeling that you need to clean them, as if you were criticizing their abilities. Despite this, you are going to need to cut their fur during certain times of the year, and they do need the occasional bath.

Starting a regular grooming session when your Shiba Inu is a puppy will make it a much easier task down the road. Since they have allergies, it is common for Shiba Inu to have problems with their coats. Regular grooming will help you to detect a potential problem early on.

Given their popularity, you can find a lot of extra advice online. This chapter provides a baseline for making sure your Shiba Inu's coat is clean and healthy, but feel free to look for additional ways to make the coat really shine if you have the time to do some additional care.

Grooming Tools

You don't need too many tools to properly groom your Shiba Inu. Make sure you have the following items on hand before your puppy or adult dog arrives:

- A bristle or pin brush for his coat
- Undercoat brush or undercoat rakes (this item is optional, but can help reduce shedding)

- Shampoo (check Barkspace for the latest recommendations for a breed with potential skin conditions) – use mild shampoos
- Nail trimmers
- Toothbrush and toothpaste (check the American Kennel Club for the latest recommendations)

Photo Courtesy of
Pervie Villareal

Coat Management

While weekly brushing is strongly recommended to keep the shedding down, if you start grooming when your puppy is young, it won't be quite the chore when he is grown. This is fantastic considering how much time you will spend with other tasks, particularly exercise and training. During the shedding seasons, you will want to brush his coat a little more often to help reduce how much fur you have blowing around your home.

Puppies

When they are puppies, Shiba Inu' coats are fairly easy to manage. Daily brushing not only can reduce how much your puppy sheds, but it helps you to build a bond with the puppy. Yes, it will be a bit challenging in the beginning because puppies don't sit still for long periods of time. There will be a lot of wiggling and attempts at play. Trying to tell your puppy that the brush is not a toy clearly isn't going to work, so be prepared to be patient during each brushing session.

On the other hand, your pup will be so adorable, you probably won't mind that it takes a bit longer. And this will be one of the only times when letting your pup sit in your lap won't put your legs to sleep (he will probably try to do it when he's older, so enjoy it while it lasts). Just make sure you let your pup know that this is a serious effort and playing comes after grooming. Otherwise, your Shiba Inu is going to always try to play, which will make brushing him a lot more time consuming – potentially

on the verge of impossible given how big he will be when he gets to be 24 months old. Plan to brush your puppy after a vigorous exercise session so that your Shiba Inu has far less energy to fight or play.

FURTHER READING
Rhyming Shiba Adventures

Did My Shiba Follow You Home Today? is a rhyming children's story geared towards children ages 4-7. The story is told from the perspective of a young girl who believes that her Shiba Inu has escaped from her backyard. This book was published in 2015 by Trafford.

You also need to get your puppy accustomed to drying his fur. With such a thick coat, you need to make sure that there isn't a lot of excess water trapped in the second coat. Encourage your puppy to shake after the bath, then towel him dry. Continue to praise your puppy while you do this, and allow for a few extra shaking sessions to bring water up to the surface. If you have the time and want to use a blow dryer, you can do that using the setting for low to medium heat, but be careful not to over dry any part of the coat.

Adult Dogs

"A correct coat is very water repellent, but if they do get wet to skin, important to get dry to avoid fungal/hot spot issues. Do not use coats, as they hold in heat and moisture. Shibas do not need artificial weather proofing - they were developed as hardy outdoor hunters."

Susan Norris-Jones
SunJo Shiba Inu & Japanese Chin

Brushing weekly is recommended because of how much Shiba Inu shed; they have two coats, so they will shed during the spring and fall when the weather changes. If you properly train your puppy how to behave, brushing him will be easy when he is an adult.

If you rescued an adult, it may take a little while to get the dog used to being brushed frequently. If you aren't able to get your dog to feel comfortable with the brushing in the beginning, you can work it into your schedule, like training.

Keep up with the same drying routine to ensure that your dog's coat doesn't have too much water left in it after the bath.

Senior Dogs

Like exercise sessions, grooming will need to be more often for shorter periods of time. Brushing every 2 or 3 days and targeting a different part of the body will help to keep your dog's coat well-groomed without making him stand up for long periods of time. Use a softer brush with plastic pins at the end of the bristles because these are softer on your dog's skin.

Grooming sessions are a good way to check for issues while giving your older pup a nice massage to ease any pain, as well as being a great way of having dedicated time together. While brushing your dog, look for any changes to the skin, such as bumps or fatty lumps. These may need to be mentioned to the vet during a regular visit if they're very large.

Allergies

If your Shiba Inu is suffering from hot spots or if you notice his coat thinning out during grooming sessions, watch for these other problems, which could be a sign of allergies:

- Wounds take longer to heal
- Weak immune system
- Aching joints
- Hair is falling out
- Ear infections

The regular brushing ensure that you are more aware of the state of your Shiba Inu's coat, which can help you more quickly identify when you pup is suffering from allergies. If you notice these issues, take your Shiba Inu to the vet.

Bath Time

"Do not bathe frequently – the Shibas skin is not oily and can get dried out."

Susan Norris-Jones
SunJo Shiba Inu & Japanese Chin

Given Shiba Inu' size and short coats, a bath every three months should be more than enough to keep your pup clean, especially if you're brushing him weekly. Set your bath schedule for about once a quarter (four times a year), and your dog should be happy. Of course, if your Shiba Inu gets dirty (which may happen whenever you go out exploring or hiking), then you'll need to take the time to bathe your canine after each of these events. Make sure the water isn't cold or hot, but comfortably warm.

1. Get everything you will need in one place before you start, then verify that you have everything before you get your Shiba Inu. At a minimum, you need the following:

    a. Shampoo and conditioners

    b. Cup for pouring water (if bathing in a tub)

    c. Towels

    d. Brushes for after the drying process

    e. Non-slip tub mat if you use a tub

Photo Courtesy of
Instagram@nova.inu

If you bathe your dog outside, you will need buckets and other items.

2. Take your Shiba Inu out for a walk. This will both tire your dog and make him a little hotter, which will make the bath less hated – maybe even appreciated.

3. Run the water, making sure that the temperature is lukewarm, but not hot, especially if you have just finished a walk. If you are washing in a bathtub, you only need enough to cover up to your pup's stomach. Do not fully cover your dog's body.

4. Pick up your dog and talk in a strong confident voice – don't baby talk, your Shiba Inu needs a confident leader, not to be treated like an infant.

5. Place the dog in the tub and use the cup to wash the dog. Don't use too much soap – it isn't necessary.

6. Talk to your dog while you are bathing him, keeping in mind you need to talk with confidence, not a high tone.

7. Make sure you don't get water in your dog's eyes or ears. You don't need to get water on the top of your dog's head. Use a wet hand and gently scrub, don't pour water on your dog's head.

8. Take your Shiba Inu out and towel him dry. You will need to take a good bit of time to do this because of the double coat.

9. Brush your dog when you are done.

Photo Courtesy of
Alayne Levine

You can use these practices with other kinds of bathing, such as outside or at a public washing facility, modifying them to the tools you have at hand.

The first few times you bathe your dog, pay attention to the things that bother or scare your dog. If he is afraid of running water, make sure you don't have the water running when your dog is in the tub. If he moves a lot when you start to apply the shampoo, it could indicate the smell is too strong. You need to modify the process to make it as comfortable for your dog as possible.

Keep in mind that you have to be patient and calm during the bath. If you get upset or take out your frustration on your dog, it will make all future baths that much more difficult as your dog will begin to stop trusting you. This isn't a fight for dominance, it is an honest lack of understanding for why you are torturing your dog when he already does so much to clean himself. Keep a calm, loving tone as you wash your dog to make it a little easier next time. Sure, your Shiba Inu may scream, throw a tantrum, or wiggle excessively, but the better you take it, the more the dog will learn that it is simply a part of being in the pack.

Cleaning Eyes And Ears

When you bathe your Shiba Inu, be careful not to get water in his ears. You should also make a habit of checking his ears once a week to make sure they're healthy. He may have allergies that make the inside of his ears look red. A warm, moist pad can be used on the surface part of the ear. If the redness doesn't look better in a day, make an appointment to visit the vet. If you see wax buildup, you can very gently wipe it away. Never put anything in your dog's ears though.

Shiba Inu have several genetic eye conditions (Chapter 17), so take the time to always check your dog's eyes while you are grooming him. Cataracts are a fairly common problem for all dogs as they age. If you see cloudy eyes, have your Shiba Inu checked. If he's developing cataracts, you may need to take the pup in to have them removed because cataracts can lead to blindness.

Trimming Nails

"Nails can be a big issue with Shibas - they feel trapped when paws are held. Start young, and tip nails every week. Using a Dremel is often better tolerated (caution that drums can get hot and burn- there is a diamond drum available that stays cool)."

Susan Norris-Jones
SunJo Shiba Inu & Japanese Chin

Cutting Shiba Inu' nails can difficult because some have black nails or it can be difficult to tell how much is too much, which means that you may cut too much off and cause the quick to bleed. It's best to have an expert cut your dog's nails until you can see how it's done. If you have not cut a dog's nails before, you need to learn from a professional as the nails can bleed a lot if done wrong. Since it can be difficult to tell how far to go on a Shiba Inu's nails, you need to learn from an expert before you try it yourself. If you already know how to cut a dog's nails, make sure to have some styptic powder nearby in case you cut too much off.

To know when your pup needs his nails cut, pay attention when your dog is walking on hard surfaces to make sure his nails aren't clicking. If they are, then you should increase how often you get your dog's nails trimmed. As a general rule, once a month is recommended.

Oral Health And Brushing Your Dog's Teeth

Shiba Inu need their teeth brushed often to avoid dental problems, and you probably will want to learn to do it yourself over having to visit a shop once a week. It's also nice to know how to do it if his breath smells bad or he eats something that smells foul.

Again, you have to learn to be patient and keep it from being an all-out fight with your dog. Firm and consistent with a healthy helping of patience is the way to get a Shiba Inu to finally come around to doing things your way. They are always going to look for ways to get what they want, so you have to let them know that there is no way around brushing, but it isn't a threatening activity.

Always use a toothpaste that is made for dogs. Human toothpaste can be toxic. The flavor of dog toothpaste will also make it easier to brush your dog's teeth – or at least entertaining as he tries to eat it. To start brushing your pup's teeth:

1. Put a little toothpaste on your finger and hold it out to your dog.

2. Let your dog lick the toothpaste.

3. Praise your dog for trying something new.

4. Put a little toothpaste on your finger, lift up your dog's upper lip, and begin to rub in circles along your Shiba Inu's gums. Your pup will very likely make it difficult by constantly trying to lick your finger. Give your puppy praise when he doesn't wiggle too much.

   a. Try to move in a circular motion. This will be very tricky, especially with those sharp baby teeth.

   b. Try to keep the puppy still without putting the little pooch in a vise. As your puppy gets bigger, you'll need for him to know how to sit for the cleaning voluntarily.

   c. Try to massage both the top and bottom gums. It is likely that the first few times you won't be able to do much more than get your finger in your dog's mouth, and that's okay. Over time, your puppy will learn to listen as training elsewhere helps your dog understand when you are giving commands.

5. Stay positive. No, you probably won't be able to clean the puppy's teeth properly for a while, and that is perfectly fine so long as you keep working at it patiently and consistently.

Once your dog seems all right with you brushing his teeth with your finger, try the same steps with a toothbrush. It may be a similar song and dance in the beginning, but it shouldn't take nearly as long. It could take a couple of weeks before you can graduate to a toothbrush, but even if it does take that long, it's still great bonding time.

CHAPTER 16
General Health Issues: Allergies, Parasites, And Vaccinations

Environmental factors largely determine whether or not your dog gets parasites. For example, if you live near a wooded area, your dog is at a greater risk of ticks than a dog that lives in the city. Talk to your vet about particular environmental risks to your dog.

The Role Of Your Veterinarian

From getting annual vaccines updated to health checkups, regularly scheduled vet visits will make sure that your Shiba Inu stays healthy. Since Shiba Inu can be somewhat indifferent to attention, you may find it a bit more difficult to tell when he isn't feeling well, until it is time to do something exciting. If your Shiba Inu doesn't seem as excited as usual about walking, hiking, or other activities that he normally enjoys, then it is likely he doesn't feel well. Annual visits to the vet will ensure there isn't a problem that is slowly draining the energy or health from your dog.

Health checkups also make sure that your Shiba Inu is aging well. If there are any early symptoms of something potentially wrong with your

dog over the years (such as arthritis), an early diagnosis will allow you to start making adjustments early. The vet can help you come up with ways to manage pain and problems that come with the aging process and will be able to recommend adjustments to the schedule to accommodate your canine's aging body and diminishing abilities. This will ensure that you can keep having fun together without hurting your dog.

Photo Courtesy of Jerry Simek

Vets can provide treatments and/or preventive medications for the different parasites and microscopic threats that your dog may encounter when he is outside, during interactions with other dogs, or from exposure to animals outside your home.

Allergies

Like people, dogs can have allergies, and Shiba Inu are often affected by this problem. The problem is that it can be difficult to tell when a dog is having an allergic reaction. The scientific name for environmental allergies is atopic dermatitis, but it's more difficult to tell whether the problem is with the environment or the food you're giving your dog. The symptoms tend to be similar in dogs for both types of allergies:

- Itching/scratching, particularly around the face
- Hot spots
- Ear infections
- Skin infections
- Runny eyes and nose (not common)

Grooming your dog is a great time to pay attention to many of these potential problems.

Dogs often develop allergies when they are between 1 and 5 years old. Once they develop allergies, canines don't outgrow the problem. Usually dog allergies are related to skin exposure, but some canines can be allergic to inhaling microscopic particles, such as dust, molds, and pollens.

Since the symptoms are the same for food and environmental allergies, you will need to talk to your vet about determining the cause. If your dog has a food allergy, all you have to do is change the food that you give him. If he has an environmental allergy, he will need medication, just as humans do. Because of this, you will want to know if the problem is from something seasonal (like pollen) or something year round so you will know when to treat your dog.

As with humans, completely eliminating the problem really isn't reasonable – there is only so much you can do to change the environment around your dog. There are several types of medications that can help your dog become less sensitive to the allergens.

- Antibacterials/Antifungals – Shampoos, pills, and creams usually do not treat the allergy, but the problems that come with allergies, such as bacterial and yeast infections.

- Anti-inflammatories – These are over-the-counter oral medications that are comparable to allergy medicine for people. You will need to be careful if you use these medications, monitoring your dog to see if he has any adverse effects. Don't start to give your dog any medication without first consulting with the vet. If your dog has a bad reaction, such as lethargy, diarrhea, or dehydration you should consult with your vet.

- Immunotherapy – A series of shots can help reduce your dog's sensitivity to whatever he is allergic to. This is something you can do at home, so you won't need to take your dog to the vet to complete the series. Learn how to give the shots from your vet, and then you can find out how to get the shots for your area. Scientists are also developing an oral version of the medication to make it easier to take care of your dog.

- Topical – This medication tends to be a type of shampoo and conditioner that will remove any allergens from your dog's fur. Giving your dog a warm (not hot) bath can also help relieve itching.

Talk with your vet about the medications that are available for your dog to determine the best treatment for your situation and your Shiba Inu's needs.

Inhalant And Environmental Allergies

Inhalant allergies are caused by things like dust, pollen, molds, and even dog dander. A dog's reaction tends to be different than a person's reaction. Instead of sneezing and having a runny nose, dogs tend to itch more because of the allergy. Your dog might scratch at a particular hot spot or he might start to paw at his eyes and ears. Some dogs do have runny noses and sneeze prolifically, but this is usually in addition to scratching.

Contact Allergies

Contact allergies mean that your dog has touched something that triggers an allergic reaction. Things like wool, chemicals in a flea treatment, and certain grasses can trigger irritation in a dog's skin, even causing discoloration. If left untreated, the allergic reaction can begin emitting strong odors and cause fur loss.

Like food allergies, contact allergies are easy to treat because once you know what is irritating your dog's skin, you can remove the problem.

Fleas And Ticks

Given how much Shiba Inu love to be outdoors, they're at a much greater risk of both ticks and fleas than many other dogs, and neither parasite is easy to see because a Shiba Inu has a dark coat. Therefore, you can't allow any lapse in anti-flea and tick treatment, even in the winter.

Make it a habit to check for ticks after every outing into the woods, or near long grass or wild plants. Comb through your dog's fur and check his skin for irritation and parasites. Since you will be doing this often, you should be able to notice when there's a change, such as a new bump, for example. Since your dog will be very happy to spend time with you, the skin check shouldn't take long.

Fleas are problematic because they're far more mobile than ticks. The best way to look for fleas is to make it a regular part of your brushing sessions. You can also look for behavioral indicators, such as incessant scratching and licking. You will need to use flea preventative products on a regular basis once your puppy reaches an appropriate age.

The FDA has issued a warning about some store bought treatments. Whether you look into purchasing treatments that have to be applied monthly or a collar for constant protection, you need to check the treatment to see if it contains isoxazoline (included in Bravecto, Nexgard, Credelio, and Simparica) because this ingredient can have an adverse effect on pets. While other ingredients are safe for pets when used in the proper doses, if you use a product that is meant for a larger dog, it can be toxic to your dog. Consult with your vet about recommended treatments to ensure that you get the right dose of flea and tick repellant for your dog's size and needs. When you start applying the treatment, monitor your dog for the following issues:

- Diarrhea/vomiting
- Trembling
- Lethargy
- Seizures

Take your dog to the vet if you notice any of these issues.

Never use any product designed for a dog on a cat or vice versa. If your dog is sick, pregnant, or nursing, you may need to look for an alternative treatment. Flea collars are generally not recommended because they are known to cause problems in pets and people. If you have a cat or young children, you should choose one of the other options for keep-

ing fleas and ticks off of your dog. This is because flea collars contain an ingredient that is lethal to felines and which is believed might be carcinogenic to humans.

When you purchase a flea treatment, make sure to read the packaging to find out when is the right time to begin treating your dog based on his current age and size. Different brands have different recommendations, and you don't want to start treating your puppy too early. There are also very important steps to apply the treatment. Make sure you understand all of the steps before you purchase the flea treatment.

If you want to use natural products instead of chemical ones, set aside a few hours to research the alternatives and find out what works best for your Shiba Inu. Verify that any natural products work before you buy them and make sure you consult with your vet. Establishing a regular schedule and adding it to the calendar will help you remember to consistently treat your dog each month.

Photo Courtesy of Cheryl Carleton

Parasitic Worms

Although worms are a less common problem than fleas and ticks, they can be far more dangerous. Your dog can become sick from worms that are carried by fleas and ticks. There are a number of types of worms that you should be aware of:

- Heartworms
- Hookworms
- Roundworms
- Tapeworms
- Whipworms

Unfortunately, there isn't an easy-to-recognize set of symptoms to help identify when your dog has worms. However, you can keep an eye out for these symptoms, and if your dog shows them, schedule a visit to the vet.

- Your Shiba Inu is unexpectedly lethargic for at least a few days.
- Patches of fur begin to fall out (this will be noticeable if you brush your Shiba Inu regularly) or if you notice patchy spaces in your dog's coat.
- Your dog's stomach becomes distended (expands) and looks like a potbelly.
- Your Shiba Inu begins coughing, vomiting, has diarrhea, or has a loss in appetite.

If you aren't sure about any symptom, it's always best to get to the vet as soon as possible to check.

Heartworms

Heartworms are a significant threat to your dog's health and can be deadly as they can both slow and stop blood flow. You should be actively treating your dog for heartworm protection to ensure that this parasite does not have a home in your dog.

Fortunately, heartworms are among the easiest health problems to prevent. There are medications that can ensure your Shiba Inu does not get heartworms. To prevent this very serious problem, you can give your dog a chewable medication, topical medicine, or you can request shots.

This particular parasite is carried by mosquitoes, which are nearly impossible to avoid in most regions of the country. Since heartworms are potentially deadly, taking preventative measures is essential.

If a dog has heartworms, the condition is costly and time-consuming to treat and cure, but it will be well worth all of the work because of how amazing the dogs are.

1. The vet will first draw blood to conduct tests, which can cost as much as $1,000.

2. Treatment will begin with some initial medication, including antibiotics and anti-inflammatory drugs.

3. Following a month of the initial medication, your vet will give your dog three shots over the course of two months.

From the time when the vet confirms that your dog has heartworms until he or she says your dog is clear of the parasite, you have to keep your dog calm. Your vet will tell you how best to exercise your canine during this time. Considering your Shiba Inu is likely to be energetic, this is going to be a very rough time for both you and your dog. You will need to be careful when your dog exercises because the worms are in your dog's heart, inhibiting blood flow. Therefore, getting your dog's heart pumping too much can kill him.

Treatment will continue after the shots are complete. After about 6 months, your vet will conduct another blood test to ensure that the worms are gone.

Once your dog is cleared of the parasites, you will need to be vigilant about medicating your dog against heartworms. You want to make sure that your poor little guy doesn't suffer through that again. There will be lasting damage to your dog's heart, so you will need to ensure that your dog does not over exercise.

Intestinal Worms: Hookworms, Roundworms, Tapeworms, And Whipworms

All four of these worms thrive in your dog's intestinal tract, and they get there when your dog eats something contaminated with them. The following are the most common ways that dogs ingest worms:

- Feces
- Small hosts, such as fleas, cockroaches, earthworks, and rodents
- Soil, including licking it from their fur and paws
- Contaminated water
- Mother's Milk (if the mother has worms, she can pass it to young puppies when they eat)

The following are the most common symptoms and problems caused by intestinal parasites:

- Anemia
- Blood loss
- Coughing
- Dehydration
- Diarrhea
- Large intestine inflammation
- Weight loss

If a dog rests in soil with hookworm larvae, the parasite can burrow through the canine's skin. Vets will conduct a diagnostic test to determine if your dog has this parasite. If your dog does have hookworms, your vet will prescribe a de-wormer. You should visit a doctor yourself because humans can get hookworms, too.

Roundworms are kind of like fleas in that they are very common, and at some point in their lives, most dogs have to be treated for them. They primarily eat the digested food in your dog's stomach, getting the nutrients that your dog needs. It is possible for larvae to remain in your dog even after all of the adult worms have been eradicated. Mothers can pass these larvae to their puppies. This means if you have a pregnant Shiba Inu, you will need to have her puppies periodically checked to make sure the inactive larvae aren't passed on to the puppies. The mother will also need to go through the same testing to make sure they don't make her sick. In addition to the symptoms listed above, your Shiba Inu may appear to have a potbelly. You may also see the worms in your dog's excrement or vomit.

Tapeworms are usually eaten when they are eggs, usually carried by fleas or from the feces of other animals that have tapeworms. They develop in the canine's small intestine until they are adults. Over time, parts of the tapeworm will break off and become obvious in your dog's waste, which needs to be carefully cleaned up to keep other animals from getting tapeworms. While tapeworms typically aren't fatal, they can cause weight loss while giving your dog a potbelly (depending on how big the worms get in your dog's intestines).

Your vet can test your dog to see if he has tapeworms, and will prescribe a medication that you can give your dog, including chewables, tablets, or a medication you can sprinkle on your dog's food. There is a low risk of humans getting tapeworms, with kids being at the greatest risk because of the likelihood that they will play in areas where there is dog waste and then not wash their hands carefully enough afterward. It is possible to contract tapeworms if a person swallows a flea, which is possible if your dog and home have a serious infestation.

Whipworms grow in the large intestine, and in large numbers they can be fatal.

FURTHER READING
The Forgotten Shiba

The Forgotten Puppy, published in 2018, is part of the Pet Rescue Adventures children's book series published by Tiger Tales. This installment tells the story of an adopted Shiba Inu puppy named Miki and her owner, Emi. The real adventure begins when Miki gets out while Emi is away with her dad. Will the duo be reunited? Read the book to find out!

*Photo Courtesy Of
Sophie Riggs*

Their name is indicative of their appearance, with their tails appearing thinner than the upper section. Like the other worms, you will need to have your dog tested to determine if he appears to be sick.

Keeping up with flea treatments, making sure people pick up behind their pets, and watching to make sure your Shiba Inu doesn't eat trash or animal waste are the best preventative measures to keep your dog safe from getting these parasites.

If your dog has hookworms or roundworms, these can be spread to you from your dog through skin contact. Being treated at the same time as your Shiba Inu can help stop the vicious cycle of continually switching which of you has worms.

Preventative measures against all of these worms can be included with the preventative medication for heartworms. Talk to your vet about the different options to keep your pet from suffering any of these health problems.

Vaccinating Your Shiba Inu

Vaccination schedules are almost universal for all dog breeds, including Shiba Inu. The following list can help you ensure your Shiba Inu receives the necessary shots on schedule. Make sure to add this to your calendar. As a reminder, no shots should be administered during the first vet visit. Your new dog already has enough stress with all of the changes in his life without adding illness. If your puppy is due for more shots soon after arriving at your home, that trip should be scheduled separately, once your puppy feels more comfortable in your home.

The following table provides details on which shots should be administered and when.

Timeline	Shot		
6 to 8 weeks	Bordetella	Leptospira	DHPP – First shot
	Lyme	Influenza Virus-H3N8	Influenza Virus-H3N2
10 to 12 weeks	Leptospira	DHPP – Second shot	Rabies
	Lyme	Influenza Virus-H3N8	Influenza Virus-H3N2
14 to 16 weeks	DHPP – Third shot		
Annually	Leptospira	Bordetella	Rabies
	Lyme	Influenza Virus-H3N8	Influenza Virus-H3N2
Every 3 Years	DHPP Booster	Rabies (if opted for longer duration vaccination)	

These shots protect your dog against a range of ailments. Keep in mind that you will need to make shots an annual part of your dog's vet visits so that you can continue to keep your pup safe. If you would like to learn more about the diseases these vaccinations protect your dog from contracting, check out the Canine Journal. They provide details about the ailments and other information that can help you understand why it is so important to keep up with the shots.

Holistic Alternatives

Wanting to keep a dog from a lot of exposure to chemical treatments makes sense, and there are many good reasons why people are moving to more holistic methods. However, doing this requires a lot more research and monitoring to ensure that the methods are working – and most importantly, do not harm your dog. Unverified holistic medicines can be a waste of money, or worse, they can even be harmful to your pet.

If you decide to go with holistic medication, talk with your vet about your options. You can also seek out Shiba Inu experts to see what they recommend before you start using any methods you are interested in trying. Read what scientists have said about the medicine you are considering. There is a chance that the products you buy from a store are actually better than some holistic medications.

Make sure you are thorough in your research and that you don't take any unnecessary risks with the health of your Shiba Inu.

CHAPTER 17
Genetic Health Concerns Common To The Shiba Inu

"Shibas can have loose patellas (knee joints), causing dogs to limp in their rears, glaucoma, which can cause blindness, and hip dysplasia. Good breeders test all their breeding stock for those anomalies, so choose a conscientious, knowledgeable breeder."

CJ Strehle
JADE Shiba Inu

All pure breed dogs have genetic diseases, even the Shiba Inu. Despite this, given the fact that they have been around for millennia, they are an incredibly healthy pure breed. This is in large part because of how cautious breeders were when they brought the breed back from the brink of extinction. They also learned a valuable lesson about how best to ensure that the dogs are healthy when they are born. Good breeders offer guarantees (Chapter 3) to ensure their puppies can be returned if they have one of a particular breed's known genetic issues. To meet the requirements of these guarantees you have to know the problems and their symptoms. The sooner you start to counter any potential problems, the healthier your Shiba Inu is likely to be.

Breeders should be able to provide health records in addition to any shot records and required tests. Making sure that the parents are healthy increases the likelihood that your puppy will remain healthy over his entire life. However, there is still a chance that your dog will have one of these documented problems even if the parents don't, so you will still need to keep an eye on your friend.

As we've noted before, the most common problem for Shiba Inu is allergies. Chapter 16 provides more details on what to look for in allergies. This chapter focuses specifically on other potential hereditary problems.

*Photo Courtesy of
Kristi Wiegraffe*

Hip And Elbow Dysplasia

Hip and elbow dysplasia is a common problem for dogs, especially those that have a history of working. A dog's diet (Chapter 13) as a puppy can help minimize problems when he becomes an adult. Both types of dysplasia are a result of the dog's hip and leg sockets being malformed and that often leads to arthritis as the improper fit damages cartilage. The condition is possible to detect by the time a dog becomes an adult, using X-rays.

Dysplasia is a problem that your Shiba Inu may try to hide because he won't want to slow down. Your adult dog will walk a little more stiffly, or may pant even when it's not hot. The condition usually becomes more obvious as a dog nears his golden years, similar to how older people tend to change their gait to accommodate pain. Getting up may become more difficult as your dog ages.

While surgery is an option in severe cases, most dogs can benefit from less invasive treatment:

- Anti-inflammatory medications – talk to your vet (dogs should not have large doses of anti-inflammatory drugs on a daily basis since these can damage your dog's kidneys)

- Lower the amount of high-impact exercise your dog gets, especially on wood floors, tile, concrete, or other hard surfaces (you can move more to do things that exercise to keep him active without the jarring motions of walking and jogging on hard surfaces).

- Ingestible joint fluid modifiers, like glucosamine treats

- Physical therapy (such as hydrotherapy where your dog walks on a treadmill while in water), which you will need to discuss with your vet

- Weight loss (for dogs who are overweight or obese)

FURTHER READING
Shiba E-News

Shiba E-News is the official quarterly publication of the National Shiba Club of America (NSCA). This magazine is a benefit of membership with NSCA, but back issues may be purchased by non-members, provided the issue is at least one year old. More information about this publication, including article and ad submission information, can be found at the NSCA website, www.shibas.org.

Photo Courtesy of Inger Lise Fløtten

Patellar Luxation

The Shiba Inu may suffer from patellar luxation, which is also called slipping kneecaps. When the kneecaps are not properly fitted into the sockets, the back legs may have some minor problems. In most cases, patellar luxation is not a serious issue, and it is not known to cause much pain. However, occasionally it will require surgery to fix the repeated shift of the kneecap.

If your Shiba Inu occasionally seems to be in pain when walking or cries when out running, this could be a sign of the condition. They tend to hold up the affected leg for a short period of time trying to relieve the pain. It can be difficult to detect unless a dog has a more severe case, particular as your dog ages.

Eye Issues

"Glaucoma is a very serious and painful issue; unfortunately it is usually a late onset disease and doesn't show up until 8 years or older."

Susan Norris-Jones
SunJo Shiba Inu & Japanese Chin

Photo Courtesy of
Brooke Steinbach

The Shiba Inu's almond-shaped, brown eyes reflect their intense intelligence and calculations of the world around them, but those beautiful eyes also have several hereditary problems. Fortunately, they usually are not serious.

Entropion

Entropion is when the dog's eyelids roll inward, damaging the cornea as the eyelashes scratch it. The corrective surgery that fixes this problem can cause another eye disorder, ectropion. This is when the lower eyelid droops down so that you can see the soft pink tissue under the eye. While ectropion is not a serious problem – basset hounds live with it as a natural part of their facial structure – it does increase the likelihood of eye infections.

Microphthalmia

This is not a common problem, but on occasion, some puppies are born with small eyes, called microphthalmia. In most cases these dogs are blind, and it is unlikely that a reputable breeder would adopt out these puppies.

Fungal Ear Infections

Dogs' ears can create a dark, warm place for fungus, yeast, and bacteria to thrive. Allergies can be a major contributing factor, but all dogs are at risk for these types of infections. This is why it is absolutely essential that you do not let your dog's ears get wet during bath time, and must monitor his ear health. Watch for the following issues in your dog's ears:

- Colored discharge (particularly brown or bloody)
- Swelling and redness
- Crust forming on the skin of the ear flap
- Scratching at the ear or frequent shaking of the head
- Loss of hearing or balance
- Walking in circles (beyond the usual for bathroom inspections or nesting before lying down)

If you notice any of these symptoms, take your dog to the vet, even if the symptoms seem mild. There are a number of different available treatments, depending on the severity of the condition. Usually an antifungal cream will be recommended, but more serious problems (such as infection in the middle ear) could require injections or surgery.

Photo Courtesy of
Reagan Smith

If your dog suffers from chronic fungal ear infections, your vet will likely recommend an ear cleaner designed to prevent the problem or a solution that will keep the area dry.

Common Owner Mistakes

In addition to genetic problems, there are things that you can do that could damage your dog's health related to diet and exercise levels. In the early days, it is a difficult balance to strike as your puppy is exuberant and bouncy. Even when he is a fully grown dog, you have to make sure that you are minimizing how much stress is placed on your Shiba Inu's frame. Weight management is one important way of keeping your dog healthy. You need to ensure that your dog is getting the right nutrition for his activity level to keep him from having a greater risk of exacerbating hip and elbow dysplasia.

Failing to notice early signs of potential issues can be detrimental, even fatal. If at any point you notice strange changes in your dog's behavior, take him to the vet. As a fairly healthy breed, strange behavior in a Shiba Inu is likely a sign of something that should be checked.

Prevention And Monitoring

The recent trend of "cute" overweight Shiba Inu has called attention to the potential health risks that this kind of trend can cause. This is a breed that is already cute on its own, so you should not sacrifice your dog's health in the name of cute. Instead, take extra time to train your dog to do something cute. This is both healthier and more fun.

Monitoring your Shiba Inu's weight is important at least once a quarter or twice a year. With hip and elbow dysplasia being a real genetic problem, additional weight will only worsen things. Your vet will likely talk to you if your dog is overweight because this not only puts a strain on the dog's legs, joints, and muscles, but it can also have adverse effects on your dog's heart, blood flow, and respiratory system. Make sure to talk to your vet if you notice that your Shiba Inu is having any trouble. Those regular vet visits can help you address issues that you may not think are that big a deal. Sometimes the symptoms you notice are a sign of a future problem.

CHAPTER 18
The Aging Shiba Inu

FUN FACT
Planet's Oldest Dog

A Shiba Inu mix, named Pusuke, was the world's oldest dog from December 2010 until his death in December 2011. Pusuke was 26 years and 8 months old when he peacefully passed away in his home surrounded by family. In 2008 Pusuke was in a car accident and suffered serious injuries, but after a successful surgery went on to live out the rest of his happy life with owner, Yumiko Shinohara. The world's oldest recorded dog was an Australian cattle dog named Bluey who lived to be 29 years and 5 months old.

Most Shiba Inu live between 12 and 15 years, so you will probably have a number of really good years with your little independent sweetie. There have even been some cases when well cared for Shiba Inu lived over 2 decades – currently a Shiba Inu holds the record for the longest-lived dog (reaching 26 years old). While this is much longer than the norm, it does show that with proper care, your Shiba Inu can live a long, happy live.

At some point you will notice that your Shiba Inu is slowing down, and that is a sign that your little buddy is starting to feel the age in his bones. This usually happens at around 9 or 10 years old. A dog may remain healthy his whole life, but his body still won't be able to do the same activities as the years start to take their toll. The changes that are necessary as your dog ages will be based on your Shiba Inu's specific needs. The first signs are usually your dog's walking becoming a little stiffer or when he starts panting more heavily earlier in the walk or jog. If you see that, start to tone back the jogs, or stop jogging and just go for more energetic walks. It's likely that your Shiba Inu will want to continue to be active, which means you will need to ensure the activity levels don't stop, just make an adjustment in the kinds of activities you do.

Your schedule is going to need to change as your canine slows down. Be careful to ensure that your pup doesn't overexert himself as Shiba Inu may be too focused on being active to realize they're hurting and need to stop to rest. As an incredibly independent dog, your Shiba Inu is really not going to want to accept that things are changing and he won't be able to control it.

There is a reason these are called the golden years – you can really enjoy them with your dog. You don't have to worry as much about him tearing things up out of boredom or getting overexcited on walks any-more. You can enjoy lazy evenings and peaceful weekends with some less strenuous exercise to break up the day. It's easy to make the senior years incredibly enjoyable for your Shiba Inu and yourself by making the necessary adjustments.

Senior Care Challenges

In most cases, caring for an older dog is much simpler than taking care of a younger dog, and Shiba Inu are no exception.

Accommodations you should make for your senior Shiba Inu include:

- Set water bowls out in a couple of different places so that your dog can easily reach them as needed.
- Cover hard floor surfaces (such as tile, hardwood, and vinyl). Use non-slip carpets or rugs.
- Add cushions and softer bedding for your Shiba Inu. This will both make the surface more comfortable. There are bed warmers for dogs if your

Photo Courtesy of
Cheryl Carleton

Shiba Inu displays achy joints or muscles often. Of course, you also need to make sure he isn't too warm, so this can be a fine balancing act.

- To improve his circulation, increase how often you brush your Shiba Inu.

- Stay inside in extreme heat and cold. Your Shiba Inu is hardy, but an old canine cannot handle extreme changes as well as he once did.

- Use stairs or ramps for your Shiba Inu wherever possible so that the old pup doesn't have to try to jump.

- Avoid moving your furniture around, particularly if your Shiba Inu shows signs of having trouble with his sight or has dementia. A fa-

Photo Courtesy of
Miriam Jamison

miliar home is more comforting and less stressful as your pet ages. If your Shiba Inu isn't able to see as clearly as he once did, keeping the home familiar will make it easier for your dog to move around without getting hurt.

- If you have stairs, consider setting up an area where your dog can stay without having to go up and down them too often.
- Create a space where your Shiba Inu can relax with fewer distractions and noises. Don't make your old friend feel isolated, but do give him a place to get away from everyone if he needs to be alone.
- Be prepared to let your dog out more often for restroom breaks.

Common Physical Disorders Related To Aging

Previous chapters cover illnesses that are common or likely with a Shiba Inu, but old age tends to bring a slew of ailments that aren't particular to any one breed. Here are the things you will need to watch for (as well as talking to your vet about them).

- Arthritis is probably the most common ailment in any dog breed, and the Shiba Inu is no exception. If your dog is showing signs of stiffness and pain after normal activities, talk with your vet about safe ways to help minimize the pain and discomfort of this common joint ailment.
- Gum disease is a common issue in older dogs as well, and you should be just as vigilant about brushing his teeth when your dog gets older as at any other age. A regular check of your Shiba Inu's teeth and gums can help ensure this does not become a problem.
- Loss of eyesight or blindness is relatively common in older dogs, just as it is in humans. Have your dog's vision checked at least once a year and more often if it is obvious that his eyesight is failing.
- Kidney disease is a common problem in older dogs, and one that you should monitor for the older your Shiba Inu gets. If your canine is drinking more often and having accidents regularly, get your Shiba Inu to the vet as soon as possible and have him checked for kidney disease.
- Diabetes is probably the greatest concern for a breed that loves to eat as much as your Shiba Inu does, even with 2 hours of daily exercise most of the dog's adult life. Although diabetes is usually thought of as a genetic condition, any Shiba Inu can become diabetic if not fed and exercised properly. This is another reason why it's so important to be careful with your Shiba Inu's diet and exercise levels.

Photo Courtesy of
Ryan N Rodriguez

Steps, Ramps, And Wheelchairs

You shouldn't pick your Shiba Inu up to carry him upstairs or put him in the car – he still wants to be independent, as well as potentially doing damage when you lift him. Steps and ramps are the best way to safely ensure your Shiba Inu can maintain some level of self-sufficiency as he ages. Also, using steps and ramps provides a bit of extra exercise.

Vet Visits

As your Shiba Inu ages, you are going to notice the slow down, and the pain in your Shiba Inu's body will be obvious, just like it is in an older person. Make sure that you have regular visits with your vet to ensure that you aren't doing anything that could potentially harm your Shiba Inu. If your Shiba Inu has a debilitating ailment or condition, you may want to discuss the options for ensuring a better quality of life for him, such as wheels if your Shiba Inu's legs begin to have serious issues.

The Importance Of Regular Vet Visits And What To Expect

Just as humans go to visit the doctor more often as they age, you'll need to take your dog to see your vet with greater frequency. The vet can make sure that your Shiba Inu is staying active without overdoing it, and that there is no unnecessary stress on your older dog. If your canine has sustained an injury and hidden it from you, your vet is more likely to detect it.

Your vet can also make recommendations about activities and changes to your schedule based on your Shiba Inu's physical abilities and any changes in personality. For example, if your Shiba Inu is panting more now, it could be a sign of pain from stiffness. This could be difficult to distinguish given how much Shiba Inu pant as a rule, but if you see other signs of pain, schedule a visit with the vet. Your vet can help you determine the best way to keep your Shiba Inu happy and active during the later years.

The following are the kinds of things to expect when you go to the vet.

- Your vet is going to talk about your dog's history, even if you have visited every year. This talk is necessary to see how things have gone or if any possible problems have started to manifest themselves or have gotten worse.

- While you chat, your vet will probably conduct a complete physical examination to assess your dog's health.

- Depending on how old your dog is and the kind of health he is in, your vet may want to run different tests. The following are some of the most common tests for older dogs.
    - Arthropod-borne disease testing, which involves drawing blood and testing it for viral infections
    - Chemistry Screening for kidney, liver, and sugar evaluation
    - Complete blood count
    - Fecal Flotation, which involves mixing your dog's poop with a special liquid to test for worms and other parasites
    - Heartworm testing
    - Urinalysis, which tests your dog's urine to check the health of your dog's kidneys and urinary system
- The routine wellness check that the vet has been conducting on your dog for years
- Any breed-specific tests for your aging Shiba Inu

Changes To Watch For

Keep an eye out for different signs that your dog is slowing down. This will help you to know when to adjust the setup around your home and to reduce how much your old pup is exercising.

Appetite And Nutritional Requirements

With less exercise, your dog doesn't need as many calories, which means you need to adjust your pup's diet. If you opt to feed your Shiba Inu commercial dog food, make sure you change to a senior food. Senior food is designed for the changing dietary needs of older dogs, with fewer calories and more nutrients that the older dog body needs.

If you make your Shiba Inu's food, talk to your vet and take the time to research how best to reduce calories without sacrificing taste. Your canine is going to need less fat in his food, so you may need to find something healthier that still has a lot of taste to supplement the types of foods you gave your Shiba Inu as a puppy or active adult dog.

Exercise

Since Shiba Inu are so gregarious, they are going to be just as happy with extra attention from you as they were with exercise when they were younger. If you make fewer demands, decrease the number of walks, or in any way change the routine, your Shiba Inu will quickly adapt to the new program. You will need to make those changes based on your dog's ability, so it's up to you to adjust the schedule and keep your Shiba Inu happily active. Shorter, more frequent walks should take care of your Shiba Inu's exercise needs, as well as helping to break up your day a little more.

Your dog will enjoy napping as much as walking, especially if he gets to cuddle with you. Sleeping beside you while you watch television or as you yourself nap is pretty much all it takes to make your older Shiba Inu content, but he still needs to exercise.

The way your Shiba Inu slows down will probably be the hardest part of watching him age. You may notice that your Shiba Inu spends more time sniffing during walks, which could be a sign that your dog is tiring. It could also be his way of acknowledging that long steady walks are a thing of the past and so he is stopping to enjoy the little things more. Stopping to smell things may now give him the excitement that he used to get by walking farther.

While you should be watching for your dog to tire, he may also let you know. If he is walking slower, looking up at you, and flopping down, that could be his way of letting you know it's time to return home. If your canine can't manage long walks, make the walks shorter and more numerous and spend more time romping around your yard or home with your buddy.

Aging And The Senses

Just like people, dogs' senses weaken as they get older. They won't hear things as well as they used to; they won't see things as clearly; and their sense of smell will weaken.

The following are some of the signs that your dog is losing at least one of his senses.

- It becomes easy to surprise or startle your dog. You need to be careful because this can make your Shiba Inu aggressive, a scary prospect even in old age. Do NOT sneak up on your old dog as this can be bad for both of you, and he deserves better than to be scared.

- Your dog may seem to ignore you because he is less responsive when you issue a command. If you have not had a problem before, your dog isn't being stubborn, he is likely losing his hearing.

- Cloudy eyes may be a sign of loss of sight, though it does not mean that your dog is blind.

If your dog seems to be "behaving badly," it is a sign that he is aging, not that he doesn't care or wants to rebel. Do not punish your older dog.

Adjust your schedule to meet your dog's changing abilities. Adjust water bowl height, refrain from rearranging rooms, and pet your dog more often. He is probably nervous about losing his abilities, so it is up to you to comfort him.

Keeping Your Senior Dog Mentally Active

Just because your Shiba Inu can't walk as far doesn't mean that his brain isn't just as focused and capable. In fact, the changes in his body will probably be frustrating for him, so you want to make sure he has plenty of other things to keep him active and happy. As he slows down physically, focus more on activities that are mentally stimulating. As long as your Shiba Inu has all of the basics down, you can teach him all kinds of low impact tricks. At this point, training could be easier because your Shiba Inu has learned to focus better and he'll be happy to have something he can still do with you. That independent streak will still be there, so do give your canine options so that he can choose what he wants to do.

New toys are another great way to help keep your dog's mind active. Be careful that the toys aren't too rough on your dog's older jaw and teeth. Tug of war may be a game of the past (you don't want to hurt old teeth), but other games such as hide and seek will still be very much appreciated. Whether you hide toys or yourself, this can be a game that keeps your Shiba Inu guessing. There are also food balls, puzzles, and other games that focus on cognitive abilities. This is also a dog that loves puzzles, which makes the golden years a time for you to start coming up with ways to challenge your dog – a great mental workout for both of you.

Some senior dogs suffer from cognitive dysfunction (CCD) syndrome, a type of dementia. It is estimated that 85% of all cases of dementia in dogs go undiagnosed because of how difficult it is to pinpoint the problem. It manifests more as a problem of temperament.

If your dog begins to act differently, you should take him to the vet to see if he has CCD. While there really isn't any treatment for it, your vet can recommend things you can do to help your dog. Things like rearranging the rooms of your home are strongly discouraged as familiarity with his surroundings will help your dog feel more comfortable and will reduce stress as he loses his cognitive abilities. Mental stimulation will help to fight CCD, but you should plan to keep your dog mentally stimulated regardless of whether or not he exhibits symptoms of dementia.

Advantages To The Senior Years

The last years of your Shiba Inu's life can be just as enjoyable (if not more so) than the earlier stages since your dog has mellowed. All of those high energy activities will give way to cuddles and relaxing. Having your pup just enjoy your company can be incredibly nice (just remember to keep up his activity levels instead of getting too complacent with your Shiba Inu's newfound love of resting and relaxing).

Your Shiba Inu will continue to be a loving companion, interacting with you at every opportunity – that does not change with age. Your canine's limitations should dictate interactions and activities. If you are busy, make sure you schedule time with your Shiba Inu to do things that are within those limitations. It is just as easy to make an older Shiba Inu happy as it is with a young one, and it is easier on you since relaxing is more essential to your old friend.

Preparing To Say Goodbye

This is something that no pet parent wants to think about, but as you watch your Shiba Inu slow down, you will know that your time with your sweet pup is coming to an end. Most working dogs tend to suddenly decline, making it very obvious when you need to start taking extra care of their aging bodies. They have trouble on smoother surfaces or can't walk nearly as far as they once did. It's certainly sad, but when it starts to happen, you know to begin to prepare to say goodbye.

Some dogs can continue to live for years after they begin to slow down, but most working dogs don't make it more than about a year or two. Sometimes dogs will lose their interest in eating, will have a stroke, or other problem that arises with little warning. Eventually, it will be time to say goodbye, whether at home or at the vet's. You need to be prepared, and that is exactly why you should be making the most of these last few years.

Talk to your family about how you will care for your dog over the last few years or months of his life. Many dogs will be perfectly happy, despite their limited abilities. Some may begin to have problems controlling their bowel movements, while others may have problems getting up from a prone position. There are solutions to all of these problems. It is key to remember that quality of life should be the primary consideration, and since your dog cannot tell you how he feels, you will have to take cues from your dog. If your dog still seems happy, there is no reason to euthanize him.

Photo Courtesy of
Miriam Jamison

At this stage, your dog is probably very happy just sleeping near you for 18 hours a day. That is perfectly fine as long as he still gets excited about walking, eating, and being petted. The purpose of euthanasia is to reduce suffering, not to make things more convenient for yourself. This is what makes the decision so difficult, but your dog's behavior should be a fairly good indicator of how he is feeling. Here are some other things to watch to help you evaluate your dog's quality of life:

- Appetite
- Drinking
- Urinating and defecation
- Pain (noted by excessive panting)
- Stress levels
- Desire to be active or with family (if your dog wants to be alone most of the time, that is usually a sign that he is trying to be alone for the end)

Talk to your vet if your dog has a serious illness to determine what the best path forward is. They can provide the best information on the quality of your dog's life and how long your dog is likely to live with the disease or ailment.

If your dog gets to the point when you know that he is no longer happy, he can't move around, or he has a fatal illness, it is probably time to say goodbye. This is a decision that should be made as a family, always putting the dog's needs and quality of life first. If you decide it is time to say goodbye, determine who will be present at the end.

Once at the vet's office, if you have decided to euthanize the dog, you can make the last few minutes very happy by feeding your dog the things that he couldn't eat before. Things like chocolate and grapes can put a smile on his face for the remaining time he has.

You can also have your dog euthanized at home. If you decide to request a vet to come to your home, be prepared for additional charges for the home visit. You also need to determine where you want your dog to be, whether inside or outside, and in which room if you decide to do it inside.

Make sure at least one person he knows well is present so that your dog is not alone during the last few minutes of his life. You don't want your dog to die surrounded by strangers. The process is fairly peaceful, but your dog will probably be a little stressed. He will pass within a few minutes of the injection. Continue to talk to him as his brain will continue to work even after his eyes close.

Once your dog is gone, you need to determine what to do with the body.

- Cremation is one of the most common ways of taking care of the body. You can get an urn or request a container to scatter your dog's ashes over his favorite places. Make sure you don't dump his ashes in places where that is not permitted. Private cremation is more expensive than communal cremation, but it means that the only ashes you get are from your dog. Communal creation occurs when several pets are cremated together.

- Burial is the easiest method if you have your pet euthanized at home, but you need to check your local regulations to ensure that you can bury your dog at home because this is illegal in some places. You also need to consider the soil. If your yard is rocky or sandy, that will create problems with trying to bury your pet at home. Also, don't bury your pet in your yard if it is near wells that people use as a drinking source, or if it is near wetlands or waterways. Your dog's body can contaminate the water as it decays. You can also look into a pet cemetery if there is one in your area.

Grief And Healing

Dogs become members of our families, so their passing can be incredibly difficult. People go through all of the same emotions and feelings of loss with a dog as they do with close friends and family. The absence of that presence in your life is jarring, especially with such a loving, loyal dog like the Shiba Inu. Your home is a constant reminder of the loss, and in the beginning you and your family will probably feel considerable grief. Saying goodbye is going to be difficult. Taking a couple of days off work is not a bad idea. While people who don't have dogs will say that your Shiba Inu was just a dog, you know better, and it is okay to feel the pain and to grieve like you would for any lost loved one.

Losing your Shiba Inu is also going to make a substantial change in your schedule. It will likely take a while to get accustomed to the way your schedule has shifted. Fight the urge to go out and get a new dog because you almost certainly are not ready yet.

Everyone grieves differently, so you will need to allow yourself to grieve in a way that is healthy for you. Everyone in your family will feel the loss differently too, so let them feel it their own ways. Some people don't require much time, while others can feel the loss for months. There is no timetable, so you can't try to force it on yourself or any member of your family.

Talk about how you would like to remember your pup, and make sure to listen. You can have a memorial for your lost pet, tell stories, and plant a tree in your dog's memory. If someone doesn't want to participate, that is fine.

Try to return to your normal routine as much as possible if you have other pets. This can be both painful and helpful as your other pets will still need you just as much (especially other dogs who have also lost their companion).

If you find that grief is hindering your ability to function normally, seek professional help. If needed, you can go online to find support groups in your area to help you and your family, especially if this was your first dog. Sometimes it helps to talk about the loss so that you can start to heal.

Printed in Great Britain
by Amazon

49656342R00111